WAR MUSIC

WAR MUSIC

AN ACCOUNT OF HOMER'S *ILIAD*

CHRISTOPHER LOGUE

FARRAR, STRAUS AND GIROUX   NEW YORK

Farrar, Straus and Giroux
18 West 18th Street, New York 10011

Copyright © 1981, 1991, 1995, 2003, 2005 by Christopher Logue
Copyright © 2015 by Rosemary Hill
Editor's Preface and Editor's Note copyright © 2015 by Christopher Reid
All rights reserved
Printed in the United States of America
Originally published in 2015 by Faber and Faber Limited, Great Britain
Published in the United States by Farrar, Straus and Giroux
First American edition, 2016

Library of Congress Cataloging-in-Publication Data
Names: Logue, Christopher, 1926–2011, author. | Reid, Christopher,
    1949– author. | Homer. Iliad.
Title: War music : an account of Homer's Iliad / Christopher Logue,
    Christopher Reid.
Description: First American edition. | New York : Farrar, Straus and
    Giroux, 2016.
Identifiers: LCCN 2015036482 | ISBN 9780374286491 (hardback) |
    ISBN 9780374714291 (e-book)
Subjects: LCSH: Achilles (Mythological character)—Poetry. | Trojan
    War—Poetry. | Homer—Adaptations. | BISAC: POETRY / English,
    Irish, Scottish, Welsh. | POETRY / Epic.
Classification: LCC PR6023.O38 W36 2015 | DDC 821/.914—dc23
LC record available at http://lccn.loc.gov/2015036482

Our books may be purchased in bulk for promotional, educational, or
business use. Please contact your local bookseller or the Macmillan
Corporate and Premium Sales Department at 1-800-221-7945, extension
5442, or by e-mail at MacmillanSpecialMarkets@macmillan.com.

www.fsgbooks.com
www.twitter.com/fsgbooks • www.facebook.com/fsgbooks

3 5 7 9 10 8 6 4 2

CONTENTS

Acknowledgements vii

Editor's Preface ix

WAR MUSIC

Preamble 3

KINGS

1 7

2 45

3 61

THE HUSBANDS 85

ALL DAY PERMANENT RED 139

COLD CALLS 177

WAR MUSIC

Patrocleia 223

GBH 251

Pax 277

Appendix

BIG MEN FALLING A LONG WAY 295

Editor's Note 297

Author's Notes 337

ACKNOWLEDGEMENTS

As Christopher Logue's widow, and now the trustee of his estate, I have many people to thank, principally Christopher Reid for the delicacy, perception and affection he has brought to the task of assembling and introducing the last fragmentary text.

A project that has stretched over decades, *War Music* has needed and found many supporters, critical and financial, at different stages in its development, and all should be remembered at its conclusion.

Donald Carne-Ross suggested and commissioned the first part of it for the Third Programme (BBC Radio Three) in 1959. Since then it has had the benefit of information or criticism from: Lindsay Anderson, Laurence Aston, Liane Aukin, who also directed the stage versions and later recordings, Sally Belfrage, Charles Rowan Beye, Charles Boyle, James Campbell, Ron Costley, David Godwin, Jasper Griffin, Michael Hastings, Paul Keegan, Colin Leach, Peter Levi, Ruth Padel, George Plimpton, Bernard Pomerance, Donna Poppy, Kathleen Raine, George Rapp, Stephen Spender and George Steiner.

Financial support came from or because of: Raymond Danowski, Bernard Pomerance, Bernard Stone, the Arts Council of Great Britain, the Bollingen Foundation, the Drama Department of BBC (Radio), the Society of Authors and Lord Weidenfeld.

Others who helped in various ways were: Mme Jacques Brel, Hugo Claus, Jane Feaver, Ian Hamilton Finlay, Robert Fogarty, Michael Foster of Jane's Information Group, Alastair Fowler, Jonathan Galassi, Victoria Getty, John Gross, Shusha Guppy, Melville Hardiment, Christian Hesketh, Philip Howard, Penny Jones, Oona Lahr, Joanna Mackle, Andrew Motion, Ferdinand Mount, Michael Rogers, John Simpson of the Oxford University Press, Christian Smith, Aoibheann Sweeney, Martin Taylor of the Imperial War Museum, Michael Taylor, Stephen Tumim and Kathleen Tynan.

After 1984 Christopher enjoyed particularly happy and profitable relationships with his fellow poets and editors at Faber & Faber, Craig Raine, who persuaded him to return to *War Music*, and Christopher Reid, who has seen it to its conclusion.

War Music's most enduring friend was the late Paul Getty, and I am grateful to him and to Mark Getty for their continued support, and for permission to reproduce material in the Wormsley Library.

For this collected edition my own thanks go to Matthew Hollis for overseeing it, to Martha Sprackland for assisting him and to Rob Tufnell for providing the inspiration for the cover.

Rosemary Hill

EDITOR'S PREFACE

Christopher Logue died in 2011, at the age of eighty-five. His funeral was held in London at St Paul's Church, Covent Garden, nicknamed the Actors' Church. The service ended memorably and movingly when from behind the mourners a lone trumpeter played a verse of the Victorian hymn 'What a friend we have in Jesus' – the tune to which soldiers of the First World War sang the less pious but equally yearning words, 'When this lousy war is over'. War music, indeed. And an emotionally overwhelming theatrical coup.

Perhaps at that moment it was on the minds of many in the congregation to wonder if, before his death, Logue had been able to complete his *magnum opus*, the rewriting of the *Iliad* – Homer's epic of lousy war – which had occupied him for five decades and for which he is now best known. He had not; old age and illness had prevented it; so by that reckoning this volume is incomplete.

It represents, nonetheless, a poetic achievement of the highest order. What it offers, in simple terms, is the attempt of a man who had served briefly as a soldier,* but who had never fought in battle, to understand the nature of war and to find narrative and musical expression for it. Although he used the *Iliad* as his guiding text, Logue's purpose was decidedly not to make a translation. He enters the fray more actively than any translator could have done. The given material – setting, principal characters, plot – are recognisably Homeric, but so much had to be changed if this was to become a work fit to address, however obliquely, the realities of our own bellicose era. Hence the speeded-up, frequently cinematic reimagining of scenes, both in the world of the gods and on the battlefield; hence the racy and sometimes harsh and jarring language; hence the flagrant anachronism of many of the

* See Logue's own candid account of his military service in *Prince Charming: A Memoir* (2000).

metaphors – all designed to startle us into recognition of what in Homer remains eternally true and applicable to our condition.

None of this force is lost through failure to be completed. We are lucky, in fact, that a sufficient number of passages that would almost certainly have gone into *War Music's* projected final book, *Big Men Falling a Long Way*, can be salvaged to give a broad idea of both the book's shape and its moods. These passages are collected in an appendix to this volume, along with a necessary account of editorial procedure and some notes. For the rest, we have – I can't quite say 'pure Logue', but let's call it the magnificently rich impurity that resulted when a great poet of our time measured his own powers against those of possibly the greatest poet of all.

Christopher Reid

WAR MUSIC

Preamble

Two limestone plates support the Aegean world.
The greater Anatolian still lies flat,
But half an aeon since, through silent eyes:
    'Ave!'
God watched the counterplate subside, until
Only its top and mountain tops remained
Above His brother, Lord Poseidon's, sea:

    'And that, I shall call Greece. And those,
Her Archipelago,' said He. Then turned away
To hear Apollo and the Nine perform
Of Creation, from the stage at Table Bay.

    They enter. They attend. They bow.
The Lord of Light and Mice gives them their note.
    And then they sing:

    *'In the beginning there was no Beginning,
    And in the end, no End . . .'*

KINGS

An Account of Books 1–2

1

Picture the east Aegean sea by night,
And on a beach aslant its shimmering
Upwards of 50,000 men
Asleep like spoons beside their lethal Fleet.

Now look along that beach, and see
Between the keels hatching its western dunes
A ten-foot-high reed wall faced with black clay
Split by a double-doored gate;
Then through the gate a naked man
Run with what seems to break the speed of light
Across the dry, then damp, then sand invisible
Beneath inch-high waves that slide
Over each other's luminescent panes;
Then kneel among those panes, burst into tears, and say:

'Mother,
You said that you and God were friends.
Over and over when you were at home
You said it. Friends. Good friends. That was your boast.
You had had me, your child, your only child
To save Him from immortal death. In turn,
Your friend, the Lord our God, gave you His word,
Mother, His word: If I, your only child
Chose to die young, by violence, far from home,
My standing would be first; be best;
The best of bests; here; and in perpetuity.
    And so I chose. Nor have I changed. But now –
By which I mean today, this instant, *now* –
That Shepherd of the Clouds has seen me trashed
Surely as if He sent a hand to shoo

The army into one, and then, before its eyes,
Painted my body with fresh Trojan excrement.'

Sometimes
Before the gods appear
Something is marked:
A noise. A note, perhaps. Perhaps
A change of temperature. Or else, as now,
The scent of oceanic lavender,
That even as it drew his mind
Drew from the seal-coloured sea onto the beach
A mist that moved like weed, then stood, then turned
Into his mother, Thetis', lovelost face,
Her fingers, next, that lift his chin, that push
His long, redcurrant-coloured hair
Back from his face, her voice, her words:

'Why tears, Achilles?
Rest in my arms and answer from your heart.'

The sea as quiet as light.

'Three weeks ago,' he said, 'while raiding southern Ilium
I killed the men and burned a town called Tollo,
Whose yield comprised a wing of Hittite chariots
And 30 fertile shes.
As is required
The latter reached the beach-head unassigned,
Were sorted by the herald's staff, and then
Soon after sunrise on the following day
Led to the common sand for distribution.
At which point, mother mine' – his tears have gone –
'Enter the King. No-no. Our King of kings, Majestic Agamemnon,
His nose extruded from his lionshead cowl,
Its silvered claws clasped so' – arms over chest –

'And sloping up his shoulder, thus, the mace,
The solar mace, that stands for – so I thought –
What Greeks require of Greeks:
   To worship God; to cherish honour;
To fight courageously, keeping your own,
And so the status of your fellow lords
High, mother, high – as he knows well – as he knew well –
As he came lick-lick when the best
Met to view the shes – six with infant boys at heel –
Here sniffing, pinching here, lifting a lip, a lid,
Asking his brother: "One, Menelaos, or . . . or two?"
   Then, having scanned their anxious faces with his own,
The guardian of our people outs the mace
As if it were a mop, and with its gold
Egg-ended butt, selects – before the owed –
A gently broken adolescent she
Who came – it seemed – from plain but prosperous ground.'

   'First King, first fruit,' his mother said.
   'Will you hear more, or not?' he said.
   'Dear child . . .'
   'Then do not interrupt.'

   The stars look down.
   Troy is a glow behind the dunes.
   The camp is dark.

   'Her name was Cryzia,' Achilles said.
'Less than a week
After she went through Agamemnon's gate,
Her father, Cryzez of Cape Tollomon,
The archpriest of Apollo's coastal sanctuary,
Came to the beach-head, up, between the ships,
Holding before him, outright, with both hands
An ivory rod adorned with streams of wool,

Twice consecrated to that Lord of Light.
  Pausing an instant by Odysseus' ship –
Our centrepoint – he reached the middle of the common sand,
      and,
With the red fillets blowing round his shaven head,
Waited until its banks were packed.
Then offered all, but principally
King Agamemnon and his queenless brother,
Two shipholds of amphorae filled with Lycian wine,
A line of Turkey mules,
2,000 sheepskins, cured, cut, and sewn,
To have his daughter back: plus these gloved words:

  '"Paramount Agamemnon, King of kings,
Lord of the Mainland and of Island Greece,
May God Almighty grant that you,
And those who follow you,
Demolish Troy, then sail safe home.
  Only take these commodities for my child,
So tendering your mercy to God's son,
Apollo, Lord of Light and Mice."

  '"Yes!"
  "Yes!"
  "Yes!"
  "Yes!"

  'The fighters cried,
And Yes to them – but to themselves – the lords.

  'You would have thought the matter done.
A bargain; with himself –
Well over 40 if a day –
Having had, and then released, a dozen such for general use.

But no.
Before the fourth Yes died our guardian Lord began:

   '"As my pronouncement will affect you all,
Restrain your Yessings," yes, and when we did,
   "If," he continued, "if, priest, if
When I complete the things I am about to say
I catch you loitering around our Fleet
Ever again, I shall, with you in one,
And in my other hand your mumbo rod,
Thrash you until your eyeballs shoot.
   As for your child:
Bearing by night my body in my bed,
Bearing by day my children on her knee,
Soft in the depths of my ancestral house,
If ever she sees Ilium again
She will have empty gums. Be safe – begone. For good."
   And so the priest
Prayed while he walked towards his ship
Beside the ocean's high-browed pounders as they stoop
And seethe, smothering the skittish shingle:

   '"Lord of Mice,
Whose reach makes distance myth,
In whose abundant warmth
The vocal headlands of Cape Tollomon bask,
As all my life I dressed your leafy shrine
And have, with daily holocausts,
Honoured your timeless might,
Vouchsafe me this:
For every hair upon my daughter's head
Let three Greeks die."'

   Barely a pace
Above the Mediterranean's neon edge,

Mother and child.
   And as she asks: 'And then . . . ?'
Their early pietà dissolves,
And we move ten days back.

   Long after midnight when you park, and stand
   Just for a moment in the chromium wash,
   Far off – between the river and the tower belt, say –
   The roofs show black on pomegranate red
   As if they stood in fire.

   Lights similar to these were seen
By those who looked from Troy towards the Fleet
After Apollo answered Cryzez' prayer.

   Taking a corner of the sky
Between his finger and his thumb
Out of its blue, as boys do towels, he snapped,
Then zephyr-ferried in among the hulls
A generation of infected mice.

   Such fleas . . .
   Such lumps . . .
   Watch Greece begin to die:

   Busy in his delirium, see Tek
(A carpenter from Mykonos) as he comes forward, hit –
It seems – by a stray stone, yet still comes on,
Though coming now as if he walked a plank,
Then falling off it into nothingness.
   See 30-dead in file,
Their budded tongues crystallised with green fur,
As daily to the fire-pits more cart more,

As half, maybe, incinerated half,
And sucking on their masks
The cremators polluted Heaven.

    'Home . . .'
    'Home . . .'

    Nine days.
And on the next, Ajax,
Grim underneath his tan as Rommel after 'Alamein,
Summoned the army to the common sand,
Raised his five-acre voice, and said:

    'Fighters!
Hear what my head is saying to my heart:
    Have we forgotten to say our prayers?
One thing is sure: the Trojans, or the mice, will finish us
Unless Heaven helps.
    We are not short of those who see beyond the facts.
Let them advise. High smoke can make amends.'

    He sits.

    Our quietude assents.
Ajax is loved. I mean it. He is *loved*.
Not just for physical magnificence
(The eyelets on his mesh like runway lights)
But this: no Greek – including Thetis' son –
Contains a heart so brave, so resolute, so true,
As this gigantic lord from Salamis.

    The silence thickens.
Eyes slide, then slide away, then slide again
Onto the army's eldest augur, Calchas, who
Half rose, and having said:

'The Lord of Light finds Greece abominable,'

Half sat, sat, looked about, shirked Agamemnon's eye,
Caught ten as lordly, re-arose, and said:

'Kings lose their heads, but not their memories.
Who will protect me if I say
What Agamemnon does not want said?'

'Me,'

Said Achilles,
As he stood, lifted his palms, and swore:

'This before God:
From Ethiopia to Thrace,
From Babylon to the Hesperides,
As high – as low – as Idan peaks, or the Aegean's floor,
While I am still alive and killing, no one shall touch
You, sir, or anybody here who would say why
The Lord of Light finds Greece abominable –
And, sir, no one includes our self-appointed first,
Best King, Lord Agamemnon of Mycenae.'

Then sat beside his heart, his foster-brother, and his friend,
Patroclus, lord Menotion's son,
While Calchas said (with sympathy for all):

'The sacred vermin came because,
Though offered more than due,
King Agamemnon would not give Apollo's priest
His soft-topped-eyed and squashed-mouth daughter back.
    Nor will they boil away
Until Lord Agamemnon, dueless now,

Resigns that daughter to her father's stock
With these winged words:

   "Resume your child in Heaven's name,
And may the high smoke from the sacrifice
Of this decade of snowy sheep
Propitiate the Lord of Mice and Light."'

   Low ceiling. Sticky air.
Many draw breath
As Agamemnon, red with rage, yells:

   'Blindmouth!
Good words would rot your tongue.'
   Then reads the warning in his brother's face
And says (half to himself):
   Well, well, well, well . . .
You know your way around belief.
   Then looking out:
   'Greece knows I want this girl
More than I want the father-given, free-born she
Who rules Mycenae in my place – Greek Clytemnestra.
Although, unlike that queen, the girl has not
Parted a boy to bear my honoured name,
Yet as she stitches, stands, and speaks as well,
Raised to the rank of wife, so might she suckle.'

   The army breathes again.

   'However,
As being first means being privileged,
So privilege incurs responsibility.
And my responsibility is plain:
To keep the army whole. To see it hale.
To lead it through Troy's Skean Gate.'

Again.

'Therefore,
With the addition of a Cretan bull,
The girl, who brought me happiness,
Shall be returned to Tollomon.'

Applause.

The lord of Crete, Idomeneo, starts to slip away.

'But . . .'

Then stops.

'. . . as the loss of an allotted she
Diminishes my honour and my state,
Before the army leaves the common sand
Its captain lords will find among their own
Another such for me.'

Low ceiling. Sticky air.

Our stillness like the stillness in
Atlantis when the big wave came,
The brim-full basins of abandoned docks,
Or Christmas morning by the sea.

Until Achilles said:

'Dear sir,
Where shall we get this she?
There is no pool.
We land. We fight. We kill. We load. And then –
After your firstlings – we allot.

18

That is the end of it.
We do not ask things back. And even you
Would not permit your helmet to go round.
    Leave her to Heaven.
And when – and if – God lets me leap the Wall,
Greece will restock your dormitory.'

    'Boy Achilleus,' Agamemnon said,
'You will need better words
And more than much more charm
Before your theorising lightens me.
    Myself unshe'd, and yours still smiling in the furs?
Ditchmud.'

    Widening his stare:

    'Consult. Produce a string. Or –
Now listen carefully – I shall be at your gate
Demanding Uxa, Ajax, or
At my lord Diomed's for Gwi –
Kah! – What does it matter whose prize she I take?
But take I shall, and if needs be, by force.

    'Well . . .
We shall see.

    'And now
Let us select and stow a ship,
Captained by you, lord Thoal, or by you,
Our silencer, Idomeneo.
At all events, some diplomatic lord
To take my pretty Cryzia home
That holy smoke and thermal prayers
Commend the Son of God
To exorcise the insects we refresh.'

19

'Amen . . .'

Then would have stood and gone, except
Achilles strode towards him, one arm up,
Jabbing his fist into the sky, and calling:
    'Mouth! King mouth!'
Then stopped. Then, from the middle of the common sand, said:

    'Heroes, behold your King –
Slow as an arrow fired feathers first
To puff another's worth,
But watchful as a cockroach of his own.
    Behold his cause:
Me first, me second –
And if by chance there is a little left – me third.
    Behold his deeds:
Fair ransom scanted, and its donor spurned.
The upshot – plague.
    O Agamemnon, O King Great I Am,
The Greeks who follow you, who speak for you,
Who stand among the blades for you,
Prostitute loyalty.
    To me, the Ilians are innocent.
They have not fleeced my father's countryside.
Cloud-shadowing mountains and abyssal seas
Separate them from Pythia. And half the time
You Mycenaean/Trojans seem to me
Like two bald men fighting over a comb.
    If steal is right, my King,
It was a Spartan, not a Pythic wife
Cock Paris lifted from your brother's bed.
Your hospitality that platinum maggot slimed.
Your name, not mine, he sacked. And yours, not mine,
The battles I have sited, fought, and won.

'Well . . .
We shall see.'

Indeed.
Zero to zero. Dead cells. Shredded. Gone.

'True.'
'True.'

'Since I arrived, my Lord,
I have sent 20 lesser Ilian towns
Backwards into the smoke.
But when – as is required – we distribute,
To you the delicates, to me the dottle of their loss.
Except for her, Briseis, my ribbon she,
Whose dauntless husband plus some 60
Handsome-bodied warriors I killed and burned
At Thebé-under-Ida as it burned,
And hence was given her by you lords
In recognition of my strength, my courage, my superiority –
Although you will not treat me with respect.

'Well then, my Lord,
You change the terms, I change the tense.
Let is be was. Was to the day on which,
Prince Hector dead, backlit by long-necked flames,
You lead your Greeks necklaced with spoil
Capering along the road that tops the Wall.
Because you cannot take the city without me.
Peleus' son.
Because tomorrow I sail home.'

Silence.

Reverse the shot.

Go close.

Hear Agamemnon, Lord of lords, Autarch of Argos,
Whose eminent domain includes all southern Greece:

'Many will say
Good riddance to bad rubbish.
I shall not.
    I am your King.
God called. God raised. God recognised.
    Nestor, Odysseus, Ajax,
Cretan Idomeneo, Diomed,
Thoal of Macedon, Jica of Thessaly,
Stand at my name.
    Look at them, boy. They are not muck.
They have been here nine years. When you were what? –
A bubble on a dam? And they are staying.
Likewise the thousands in whose sight we stand.
They honour me. And I am popular.
    God made you fast. Some say the fastest. And some say
More beautiful than any other man.
Indubitably He made you strong and brave.
    Please do not think of staying for my sake.
Go home. Go now.
The time has come for you to see
More of your family.
And I am confident that he will find –
And we shall hear that he has found –
More honour in the cuckoo woods of Pythia
Than he has won at Troy.'

Then to them all:

'Here is the news.
Before world-class Achilles sails,

22

As God has taken Cryzia from me
I shall take his prize she, Briseis, from him.
   More.
This confiscation shows, once and for all,
My absolute superiority,
Not just to you, retiring boy, but anyone
Stupid enough to challenge me
In word or deed.'

   Achilles' face
Is like a chalkpit fringed with roaring wheat.
His brain says: Kill him. Let the Greeks sail home.
His thigh steels flex.

   And then,
Much like a match-flame struck in full sunlight,
We lose him in the prussic glare
Teenaged Athena, called the Daughter Prince – who burst
Howling and huge out of God's head – sheds
From her hard, wide-apart eyes, as she enters
And stops time.

   But those still dying see:

   Achilles leap the 15 yards between
Himself and Agamemnon;
Achilles land, and straighten up, in one;
Achilles' fingertips – such elegance! –
Push push-push push, push Agamemnon's chest;
The King lean back; Achilles grab
And twist the mace off of him,
And lift it . . . Oh . . . flash! flash!
The heralds running up . . .
   But we stay calm,
For we have seen Athena's radiant hand

Collar Achilles' plait,
And as a child its favourite doll
Draw his head back towards her lips,
To say:

    'You know my voice?
    You know my power?

    'Be still.

    'God's wife has sent me:
"Stop him. I like them both," she said.
    I share her view.
If you can stick to speech, harass him now.
But if you try to kill him – I kill you.'

    She goes,
And time restarts.

    Achilles says:

    'I hate your voice, claw King. I hate its tune.
Lord of All Voices is God's fairest name.
Your voice defiles that name. Cuntstruck Agamemnon!
The King who would use force against his lord.
    O cheesy Lung,
I know as much, in likelihood much more,
About the use of force as any here,
Master or muster, first or flock, hero or herd,
And in my backwoods way have half a mind
To knock you multinational flat with this' –
His hand – 'then bar your throat with this' – his foot –
'Kingman who never yet led star or store
Into the blades, or kept them there,
Or raised his blade alone – for no one doubts,

24

Hector, the light of Priam's 50 sons,
Would, if you raised it, see your arm.
 Kih! I forgot. Our King is philosophical.
He fears his youth has gone. He will not fight today.
Tomorrow, then? Tomorrow we will see.
Indeed, boy Achilleus – as my dear father says –
Boy Achilleus, you are wrong to criticise.
Atreus is King. What need has he to keep
A helicopter whumphing in the dunes,
Being popular, with captains at his heel?
Although he will not stand to speak to me.'

 'Shame . . .'

 'Captains,
I was too young to take the oath you swore
When Helen's father said:
 "This womb is now a wife,"
And handed her to you, lord Menelaos.
But each to each vowed in the name of God:

 "If she, our loveliest, is stolen, or she strays,
As we are all her husbands,
Each of us, heedless of cost,
Will be in honour bound to bring her back."

 'So here you are.

 'Shame that your King is not so bound to you
As he is bound to what he sniffs.

 'Here is the truth:
King Agamemnon is not honour bound.
Honour to Agamemnon is a thing
That he can pick, pick up, put back, pick up again,

A somesuch you might find beneath your bed.
  Do not tell Agamemnon honour is
No mortal thing, but ever in creation,
Vital, free, like speed, like light,
Like silence, like the gods,
The movement of the stars! Beyond the stars!
Dividing man from beast, hero from host,
That proves best, best, that only death can reach,
Yet cannot die because it will be said, be sung,
Now, and in time to be, for evermore.'

  Amen.
  He is so beautiful.
  Without him we are lost.
Thoal, then Menelaos, then Odysseus said
(But only to themselves) as he swept on:

  'I do not fear you, King. Your voice is false.'
Then lifts his arm and makes a T –
  'You tax where you should tender, feed where fend' –
Out of its upright with the mace as bar.
  'This mace objectifies custom and truth.
Hephaestus, the Lame Lord of Fire,
Made it to glorify our Father, God,
When cosmos conquered chaos at His touch.
Mortals who tote it are required to bring
Fair judgement out of Heaven.
  By it, hear this:
Call at our gate, King, my Patroclus will
Surrender Briseis. Touch else of ours,
I will snap your back across my knee.
  And from now on,
Seeing your leadership has left me leaderless,
I shall not fight for you, or by your side,
Or for, or by, these federal lords that let you live.

Those who believe that I am in the right,
Speak now: or never speak to me again.'

No sound.

Lord Thoal thinks: Boy, boy,
You have not heard a word he said,
And in a moment you will say
Our silence has betrayed you.

Still no sound.

A whinny. Wings. The wheezing of the sea.
And so Achilles dropped the mace.

Then
Drinking his tears he called into the sky:

'Which will you see, great clouds?
Troy's topless towers fall to his voice,
Or Greece to pieces in his hands?'
    And wiping them away:
    'You lords will be his widows. Tiger bait.
Down plain, or in the dunes there, kih! –
Troy has come. Aeneas and Prince Paris come,
Moved on your Fleet by music, trumpets come,
In one wide cry of rage, Sarpedon come.
The sea will ring with it. The sea will clap its hands.
And Hector, yes, his shout alone will burst you wide.
Then neither ditch, ramp, main camp track,
Nor double row of ships that drape the bay
Headland to headland will protect your knees
As you run down the beach.
    Please do not say
"If this comes true, Achilles will relent."

Witness me glad. Yes. Glad. Extra glad when
Longing for me makes every one of you
Reach in his own broad chest,
Take out, and suck, his heart,
Then spit its extract in his neighbour's face,
Ashamed, that you, the Greek commander lords,
Dishonoured and betrayed boy Achilleus,
Promised by God, the best of the Achaeans.'

   The world is shut.

   Talthibios, chief herald of the Greeks,
Nods to a lesser indeterminate
Who lifts, then takes, the mace to Agamemnon,
Still sitting on his stool.
Then bow-backs out before their King concludes:

   'Thank you, Greece.
As is so often true,
Silence has won the argument.
Achilles speaks as if I found you on a vase.
So leave his stone-age values to the sky.'

   A few loose claps,
And those around the army's voice,
Thersites of Euboea, say
   (Not all that loudly):

   'I told you so.'
   'Shame.'
   'Home.'

   Silence again.

And as Achilles strides away without a word,
Without a word Patroclus follows him.

Low on the hillsides to the east of Troy,
Women, waist-deep in dusk, shoulder their baskets,
And, ascending, see the Wall's dark edge
Level the slopes it covers; and above, riding a lake of tiles,
The Temple on the sunset-lit Acropolis
Whose columns stripe the arrowhead
The rivers Symois and Scamander make
As they meet, whose point flows out, flows on, until,
Imagined more than seen,
King Agamemnon's army stands
(As in the sepias of Gallipoli)
Thigh-deep, chest-deep,
Out from the spits where buffalo graze,
Heaping the ocean's ember blue
Over their curls, over their shoulders, as they pray:

   'Dear Lord of Light, reclaim your mice,'

And stately through their faces, oars aloft,
Blonde Cryzia wreathed beneath its scorpion tail,
By her the bull:

   'Dear Lord of Light,'

High smoke behind them, Hesperus above,
The ship is handed south.

Moist wind. Black wind. Rainbearing wind.
The tents like lanterns; green beneath dark hulls.
    Walking between them, lower lip upthrust,
The corners of his mouth pulled down, Nestor,
The lord of Sandy Pylos,
Cloaked and calm, past 80 at a guess:
    'To see,'
Accompanied by his son, Antilochos,
    'Achilles.'

    Nod.
    Look.
    The gate.
    The compound.
    Then:
    Achilles' tent, a moonlit, Cubist, dune.

    Redcurrant hair seats white.

    Dark wine in gold.

    A sip.

    'Shame on you both.
And more on you than him.
I did not come this far to hear that Troy is innocent.
    Troy is not innocent.
    Troy lies.
    Troy steals.
    Troy harbours thieves.

    'You are the same age as my son.
He worships you. Ask him.
My sticks are cut. My place to tell you right from wrong.
    Far better men than you have seen the sky,

And I have fought beside, and saved, their like;
And I have fought against, and killed, their like;
And when the fight was done I let
Those still standing know how victors act:
And they obeyed me.
    You are a child in parliament.
Someone talks common-nonsense and – tarrah! –
You give his words a future. Let them die.
You swear; and you are sworn. The world must change.
Speak to the gods if you want change.
    Great people promise more than they perform,
And you expect too much from promising.
    Be still!
    Do not tell me Lord Agamemnon has enough.
I know Lord Agamemnon has enough.
But that is how Lord Agamemnon is.
Requiring.
    It is his due.
The mace was left to him.
He lords more men, more land, more sea
Than any other Greek.
    You are part dust, part deity.
But he is King. And so, for Greece, comes first.
    Honour his rank, honour your name.
But as Thersites' eczema words
Put off our taking Troy by putting "Home!" "Home!"
Into the army's mind, your "Home" eggs his –
And all the other gash that tumbles out
Of his sisal-ball head.
    Thersites of Euboea, blustering rat.
Peleus' son, Achilles.
To link them in a sentence is to lie.'

    Their shadows on the textile.

31

'Think of the day when I and Ajax drove
Out of the trees towards Peleus' house
And waited in its gateway while he poured
Bright wine along the thigh-cuts off a steer
Just sacrificed to God – Guardian of Kings,
The Lord of Guests – when you,
Noticing us and springing up in one,
Ran to the gateway, took our hands, and led us in.
    Kind boy. Good boy . . . And then,
When all had had enough to eat and drink,
Big Ajax asked if you, and your dear heart,
Patroclus, could join the Greeks at Troy,
And he said yes. Then eyed you up and down,
And told you: One: to be the best.
To stand among the blades where honour grows,
Where fame is won, untouched by fear,
Counting on Hera and Athene for your strength –
If they so will. And two –
Especially when Patroclus mentions it –
To mind your tongue.'

    'He also said,' Achilles said,
'That lordship knows the difference between
Anger and outrage. That the first
Is cured by time, or by revenge.
But outrage has a claim beyond itself.
That not being so, why are we here, dear father friend?'

    Gold holly in the hearth.

    'Boy,' Nestor said, 'you are my soul.
Spirit, and strength, and beauty have combined
Such awesome power in you
A vacant Heaven would offer you its throne.
    If I, your grounded honourer,

32

Persuade the King and his confederates to leave
Your she, your she, and no more said,
Will you be as you were – our edge?
    Look in my eyes, and answer.'

    Host.

    Guest.

    Patroclus – his face kept down.

    Firelight against a painted box.

    10,000 miles away
A giant child rests her chin on the horizon
And blows a city down.

    Then a new voice:

    'Father.'
    'I ordered you to wait.'
    'The King has sent Talthibios for the she.'

    The lamps lap oil.

    'Fetch her, Patroclus,' Achilles says.
And then:
    'Time-honoured lord of Pylos,
Your voice is honey and your words are winged.
I hope we meet again.'

    His awning. At its edge

    Talthibios and Kartom on their knees.

Taking their elbows.

Raising them.

'Do not embarrass me.
I know that you have no share in the blame.'

They stand. But back –
As most men do when facing him.

'Patroclus will bring her.
Tell the commanders who may ask, I meant my words.
    I hate their King. He is a needle in my bread.
He is water. I am air. I honour you. Go.
Go.'

Then, naked, walked, half walked, half trotted out
Across his compound, past its gate, its guard,
To call his mother from the sea. As we have seen.

He says:

'That is the whole of it.
The Greeks have let their King take my prize she.
And now they aim to privatise that wrong.
Make it Achilles' brain-ache, fireside, thing.
    So go to God.
Press Him. Yourself against Him. Kiss His knees.
Then beg Him this:
    Till they come running to your actual son,
Let the Greeks burn, let them taste pain,
Asphyxiate their hope, so as their blood soaks down into the sand,

Or as they sink like coins into the sea,
They learn.'

'I love you, child. But we are caught.
You will die soon. As promised. And alone.
While I shall live for ever with my tears.
Keep your hate warm. God will agree,' his mother said

And walked into the waves.
As he went up the beach towards his ship.
Towards the two great armies, all asleep.

Water, white water, blue-black here, without –
Past a turtle asleep on the sea –
Our animals hearing those closest ashore.
    Swell-water, black-water –
The breeze in the cliff pines, their hairpins, their resin,
    And –
As we glide through the cleft in the cliff's face
Goat bells greet sheep bells greet ship's bell –
    The sea is
Suddenly warm,
Refracts from its sandy floor,
As we lower, lose way, set oars – and regain it –
Whorling the shear of Tolomon's bay,
At our peak – now we ship them –
Lord Thoal's hand on her shoulder,
Cryzia, her eyes in her father's, and him –
With many – his choir, his dancers: 'Apollo!' –
His eyes in his daughter's: 'Her saviour!' —
And then, as Thoal hands her ashore:
Once more in his arms.

And when that solemn time had passed:

'Priest of Apollo's coastal sanctuary,' lord Thoal said,
'The Lord of Mainland and of Island Greece,
Paramount Agamemnon, my true King,
Bid me to lead your child into your arms.
    Thereafterwards,
That our encircling prayers
Appease the god whose vermin Greece infects,
To sacrifice these snowy sheep, this Cretan bull,
To God's first son, Apollo born,
The Lord of Light and Mice.'

The altar is oval, made of red quartz,
And broad-leaved plane trees shade the turf it crowns.
    Hear them come!
'Let the Greeks bring the knife'
    Here they come!
By the stream that freshens the bearded grass
    'To slit the Cretan bull'
Wading the orchids that verge the turf
    'And we will carry the bowls
Of mountain water and sainted wine,
And the axe.'
    'Paean!'

    See the bull at the stone
'Lord of Light!'
    See its gilded horns
'Lord of Light!'
    See the axe.

Now the lustral water is on their hands,
And the barley sprinkled on the bull's wide head.
    'Lord of Mice!'
    'Lord of Light!'
As the axe swings up, and stays,
Stays poised, still poised, and –
As it comes down:

    'PLEASE GOD!'

    'PLEASE GOD!'

Covers the terrible thock that parts the bull from its voice
As the knife goes in, goes down,
And the dewlap parts like glue
And the great thing kneels
And its breath hoses out
And the authorised butchers grope for its heart
And the choir sings:

    'Pour the oil and balm –'

And Cryzez prays:

    'O Lord of Light
    Whose reach makes distance myth,
    In whose abundant warmth
    The headlands of Cape Tollomon bask,'
            'Over the dead –'
    'As all my life I dressed your leafy shrine,'
            'Fire the cedar, fire the clove –'
    'Vouchsafe me this:'
            'That the reek may lie –'
    'Absolve the Greeks,'
            'And the savour lift –'

'Let the plague die,'
            'To Heaven, and to yourself.'
'Amen.'
'Amen.'

Were they deceived – or did
The bull consent with a shake of its head,
And the sunlight brighten, as Cryzez prayed?
Either way, the women sang:

'Child
            Child of Light
                        We beg,'

Then the men:

'Heed the thirst in our song!'

'Lord
            Lord of Light
                        We beg,'

Then the men:

'Feel the need in our song!'

And then

'Lord
            Lord of Mice
                        We pray,

'Let the plague die!
Let the plague die!'

They sang as one,
And made the day divine.

    High smoke from oil-drenched bull tripes stood in Heaven.
Leaves of lean meat spat on the barbecues.
Silver took sea-dark wine from lip to lip.
Flutes. Anklets. Acorn bells. The shameless air.
Enough for all.

    And then, when simultaneously
The moon lit this side and the sun lit that
Side of the blades they lifted to salute
The Evening Star,
Safe in Apollo's custody they slept,
Sailed on Aurora's breath
Over the shaggy waves to Troy,
And learnt the plague had gone.

  But Achilles was not glad.
Each moment of each minute of the day:
    'Let the Greeks die
    Let them taste pain'
Remained his prayer.
    And he for whom
Fighting was breath, was bread,
Remained beside his ships
And hurt his honour as he nursed his wrong.

GOD LIVES FOR EVER

Come quickly, child! There! There!
Salute Him with your eyes!
Brighter than day His shadow; silent as light
The footprint of His time-free flight
Down the Nile's length, across the Inland Sea
To Paradise Olympus where it rides
High on the snowy lawns of Thessaly,
And an unpleasant surprise is waiting for Him:

Thetis,
Wearing the beady look of motherhood,
Who starts right in:

'High King of Heaven, Whose Temple is the Sky,'
And then reminds Him of her conscientiousness;
Then (seating Him) of her enforced, demeaning coitus;
Then (as she keeps His hand) repeats
The promise He had given to her son:
    'If you, My Thetis' only child,
Choose to die young, by violence, alone,
Your honour will be recognised as best,
The best of bests,
The most astonishing that fame shall light,
Now, or in perpetuity.'
    Then (twining her arms behind His knees)
She ends:
    'I must have Yes or No.
If Yes, repeat these words:
    "In honour of Your son
Whose honour has been blighted by his King,
In that that King has grabbed his honour she,
I will take Hector's part until

The Greeks stand soaked in blood from head to foot,
Crushed by an overwhelming Trojan victory."
Then fatalise this promise with Your nod.
   If No, I am a lost bitch barking at a cloud.'

A crease has formed between God's eyes.
His silence hurts.
   Over His suppliant's tar-dark hair
He sees the ascension of the Evening Star
Beckon infinity. And says:

'Thetis, I understand. The trouble is, my wife.
Nothing delights her like abusing me.
She hates the thought of Troy.
   "So you have helped the Dribbler *again,*"
Is how she styles Priam, My best king,
A stallion man – once taken for Myself –
Who serviced 50 strapping wives from 50 towns,
Without complaint – to unify My Ilium,
Though all she says is:
   "From where I sit Your city on the hill
Stinks like a brickfield wind."
   I tell you, Hera is Greek mad.
Unable to forget that Paris judged her less –
Nudely speaking – than Lady Aphrodite.
   Better leave now. Before she sees us talking.
Have confidence. I nod. I answer: Yes.'
Adding (but only to Himself): In My own way –
And in My own good time.

   Then hitched His robe and strolled towards His court.

   Hard as it is to change the interval
At which the constellations rise
And rise, against their background dark,

Harder by far, when God inclines His head
And in the overlight His hair
Flows up the towering sky,
To vary His clairvoyance. 'Yes,'
He has said. Yes, it will be, and

    Now,
In a hoop of tidal light,
The lesser gods observing His approach,
Approach, then wait, then bow, and then,
Lit by their deferential eyes,
Conduct the King of Heaven through His park,
Enthroning Him, and, at His glance, themselves.
Except for her, His sister-wife, Queen Hera, who
Puts her face close to His, and says:

    'Warm Lord,
Have You ever seen a camel led by a crab?
If not, look here' (widening her eyes' malicious lazuli)
'And see Yourself.
Not that I am surprised. Oh dear me, no.
Who mobilised the kings? Who sent the Fleet to Troy?
But once my back is turned, plot-plot, plan-plan,
Which I, of course, will be the last to hear of.
    That salty Thetis has been at Your knee.
Not a god's god, I know. But curved.
    What did You nod to as she left?
Just because all creation knows
Fig Paris with the curly-girly hair
Refused Athena and myself, your equal self,
Does not mean You can leave us ignorant.'

    'First Heart,' God said, 'do not forget
I am at least a thousand times
Raised to that power a thousand times

Stronger than you, and your companion gods.
What I have said will be, will be,
Whether you know of it, or whether not.
Sit down. Sit still. And no more mouth.
Or I will kick the breath out of your bones.'

And Hera did as she was told.

It was so quiet in Heaven that you could hear
The north wind pluck a chicken in Australia.

And as she reached her throne she bit her tongue;
And when her son, the scientist Hephaestus, Lord of Fire –
About to dazzle Summertime
(His favourite Season) with a twisty loop
Of paradoxical diffraction foil –
Saw how upset she was, he gimped across to her and said:
    'Mother,'
But she just turned away.
    'Mother?'
Then turned the other way, and would have said:
    'Not now.
I have enough to bear without the sight of you,'
Except her mouth was full of blood.
    'Mother,' smiling his little smile, Hephaestus said:
'You are quite right to be ashamed of me,
For you are large, and beautiful, while I
Am small and handicapped.'
    And as she could not speak unless she gulped,
Just as she gulped, Hephaestus put
A jug that he had struck from frosted iron,
Then chased, in gold, with peonies and trout,
Into her hand, and said:
    'Forget God's words.
Spring kisses from your eyes.

43

Immortals should not quarrel over men.'

Then, turning on his silver crutch
Towards his cousin gods, Hephaestus
Made his nose red, put on lord Nestor's voice,
And asked:

'How can a mortal make God smile? . . .

'Tell him his plans!'

And as their laughter filled the sky,
Hephaestus lumped away remembering how,
Angered at some unwanted fact of his,
God tossed him out of Heaven into the void,
And how – in words so fair they shall for ever be
Quoted in Paradise: 'from morn
To noon he fell, from noon to dewy eve,
A summer's day; and with the setting sun
Dropped from the zenith like a falling star,
On Lemnos' in an arc that left
Him pincer-handed with crab-angled legs.

And Hera judged
The little jug's perfection with a smile,
As on God's arm, the lesser gods their train,
Starlit they moved across the lawns of Paradise,
Till them to Him, till Him to them, they bowed their might;
And soon, beside his lake-eyed queen,
God lay asleep beneath the glamorous night.

And so to Troy.

Like monumental wings
The doors that overlook the Acropolis' main court
Open onto the evening air
And Priam's portico.

And when, with Soos, his herald, to its right,
And four full-sons by either arm, his chair appears,
Neomab, Soos' next, declares:

'All rise for Priam, Laomedon's son,
Great King of Troy, the Lord of Ilium.'
He stands; some 8 foot 6; indigo skinned;
His brush-thick hair vertical to his brow blue-white.
He seats his Council of 100 with his hand,
Gathers his strength and cries:

Where is my son? My only son?
I do not see my son! He has no twin!
Take all my sons, Achilles, but not him.
(But only to himself.)

Aloud, he says:

'Blood-bound Allies –
Satraps of Thrace, of Bosphorus,
Marmarine Phrygiland and Hittite Anatolium Beyond;
    My wedded Ilians –
Cool Dardan North, dear Ida, dearest South;
    And you who come from Lycia and Cyprus:

'I reign with understanding for you all.
Trojan Antenor, being eldest, shall speak first.
    Our question is:
How can we win this war?'

    'And I reply,' Antenor says,
'How can we lose it?
    God's Troy has been besieged a dozen times
But never taken.
    Your line goes back 900 years.
The Greeks have been here nine. Surely their chance
To take our city worsens in the tenth?'
    (Anchises' face is stone.
His kinsman, Pandar, spits.)
    'If we have difficulties, so do they.
If we are tired, so are they.
And we are tired at home. Behind our Wall.
    These are their facts:
Full tents, thin blankets, gritty bread.
    And one thing more: they have a case.
Among them hospitality is sacred.
You are a guest, you are a king. The house is yours.
    Paris – may God destroy him – was Menelaos' guest.
Helen was his. She shared his rooms.
He recognised her child as his own.
He let her use the title "wife".
He wants her back. He wants her treasure back.
Neither is an unreasonable demand.
Women are property for them.
And stolen property can be returned.'

    Pandar would interrupt, but Meropt –
Aphrodité's priest – restrains him.

'My King,
The winners of a war usually get
Something out of it.
  What will we get?
Their camp. Their ditch. And who wants those?
Only Lord Koprophag, the god of filth.'

  Impatient now:

'Stand Helen on a transport floored with gold,
And as they rumble through the Skean Gate
Let trumpets from the terracing
Bray charivari to her back's bad loveliness.'

  Applause.

  And under it:

'Where can that Hector be?' the old King asks.
'On his way here, Sire. After sacrifice,' Soos says.

  As lord Antenor ends:

'Achilles is no different from the rest.
Let him face stone. Our Wall. The death of Greece.
Keep its gates down and send our allies home.
Since men have lived, they lived in Troy.
Why fight for what is won?'

  Now more – too much – applause,
Into the last of which:

'This is the why,' Anchises, lord of Ida, said,
As Pandar and Didanam
(Pandar's bow-slave) helped, then held him up:

49

For 50 years ago
As he was swimming in Gargara's lake,
Queen Aphrodité glimpsed his pretty bum,
And, while the spirits of the place looked on,
Had him on a mat of Darwin's clover.
    That done,
She pushed his hair back off his brow,
Then took his hand and spoke to him by name:

    'Anchises, I am fertile.
Our son, whom you will call *Aeneas,* shall be king.
But cite our bond to anyone but him,
And I will paralyse you from the waist downwards.'

    Gods always ask too much.
Just as Anchises said, 'This is the why,'
One day, to those who claimed that Mim –
A new-bought templemaid –
    'Is as good as Aphrodite,' he said:
    'She's not. I've had them both.'
And as they shrilled, shrivelled from hip to foot.

    Shrivelled or not:

    'This is the why,' Anchises said.
'Troy is not Ilium. And minus Ilium
Troy will not last,
    You say: "Give Helen back, they will go home."
O sorry orator, they have no home.
They are a swarm of lawless malcontents
Hatched from the slag we cast five centuries ago,
Tied to the whim of their disgusting gods,
Knowing no quietude until they take
All quiet from the world. Ambitious, driven, thieves.
Our speech, like footless crockery in their mouths.

Their way of life, perpetual war.
Inspired by violence, compelled by hate,
Peace is a crime to them, and offers of diplomacy
Like giving strawberries to a dog.'

King Priam yawns.

'They must be beaten. Preferably, destroyed.
Return their she, her boxes, they will think:
Ilium is weak – and stay. Retain them, they will think:
Ilium is fat – and stay. As either way
They want your city whole; your wives,
Your stuff and stock, floodlit by fire, while they
Pant in their stinking bronze and lick their lips.
    Ask who you like from Troy Beyond:
The Dardanelles, Negara Point,
Arisbe, Hellespont, then south,
Hac, Paran, Tollomon, and from Kilikiax
Inland as far as Thebé-under-Ida,
Seaward to Chios and to Samothrace,
All say: "For us, the time to die is ripe," and have
Nothing to spare except their injuries.
    "And where is Troy?" they ask. "We paid her well.
Priam, who had our princess for a queen,
Now turns his back, sending our allies home
As if Peleus' son was just a name."
    Ask Hector's wife. Andromache has lost
Her sire, king Etion, four brothers, and their town,
Shady Kilikiax, at Achilles' hands.
She will not underestimate the lad's ferocity.
    He is what they call Best. That is to say:
Proud to increase the sum of human suffering;
To make a wife, a widow; widows, slaves;
Hear, before laughter, lamentation;
Burn before build.

Our only question is:
How best to kill him? Pandar has planned for that.
    The saying goes:
Not the dog in the fight but the fight in the dog.
And you, Antenor, like your sons, lack fight.
You speak from cowardice. You plan from fear.'

    Then Pandar's 'True!' was mixed with someone's 'Shame . . .'
'Shame . . .' merged with 'Answer him . . .' and 'Stand . . .'
With 'Heaven sent . . .' and '. . . let her go.'
Their voices rising through the still, sweet air

    As once, as tourists, my friends and I
    Smoked as we watched
    The people of the town of Skopje
    Stroll back and forth across their fountained square,
    Safe in their murmur on our balcony
    At dusk, not long before an earthquake tipped
    Themselves and their society aside.

    Now,
Almost by touch, the Council's tumult died, as
Down the flight of steps that join
The Temple's precinct to the court,
Surrounded by Troy's dukes, Prince Hector comes.

    Whether it is his graceful confidence,
His large and easy legs, his open look,
That lets him fortify your heart,
And makes you wish him back when he has gone,
Trusting oneself to him seems right; who has belief,
And your belief respected, where he stands.

    'My son!'

No sound aside from Priam's cry, as Hector led
Chylabborak, Andromache's one brother left, king Etion's heir,
Prince Abassee, his favourite, full brother, down,
Across the courtyard, plus
  Lord Prince Aeneas,
Brave, level-headed, purposeful –
My Lady Aphrodité's child –
To whom Mount Ida's cowboys prayed:
  Troy's Lycian allies,
Gray, beside his prince, Sarpedon,
Anaxapart, Sarpedon's armourer:
  And more –
As valiant, as keen for fame, the plumes of Ilium –
That you will meet before they die,
Followed their Hector up onto the portico,
Before the monumental wings, and stood
Around the King, who pulls his son's face down
And kisses it, even as he whispers:
  'Where have you *been?*'

And Hector lets the smile this brings
Fade from his lips, before he says:

  'My friends,
Your faces bear your thoughts. Change them for these:
  My name means "He who holds."
Troy; Ilium; Troy Beyond; one thing.
  The victory is God's.

  'Anchises harms the truth
By making it offensive.
  Antenor hides the truth
By making out that Greece has lost.
  True: Raphno of Tus arrived today
With fifteen hundred extra men.

53

Yes, yes. And, yes: my father's Ilian relatives and I
Could hold Troy on our own.
God break the charm of facts.
Excepting: we are tired of our Wall.
Of waking up afraid. Of thinking: Greece.
Your life in danger all your life. Never to rise alone
Before the birds have left their nests,
Then ride alone through sunlit, silent woods,
Deep snow to spring flowers in a single day,
And then, the sea . . .
To miss these things,
When things like these are your inheritance,
Is shameful.

'We are your heroes.
Audacious fameseekers who relish close combat.
Mad to be first among the blades,
Now wounded 50 times, stone sane.
Achilles' name, that turns you whiter than a wall,
Says this: although his mother is a god,
He is a man, and like all men, has just one life,
Can only be in one place at one time.

'Fate's sister, Fortune, favours those who keep their nerve.
I know it is the plain that leads
Us to their ships, and them into the sea.
And when God shows the moment we should strike
I will reach out for it.
But I –
Not you, Anchises, and not you, Antenor –
Will recognise that moment when it comes.

'All captains to their towers.
Sleep tight. But do not oversleep.'

Did our applause delay him?
Out of the corner of his eye, Chylabborak
Sees a strange herald cross to Neomab and Soos,
Then Soos make not-now signs to Neomab,
Then Neomab, apologising with a shrug,
Go to Priam and his dukes, who ring him, and
(While our silence holds) listen, then nod.
Then face ourselves as Soos declares:

'Cryzez of Tollomon sends this news:
Achilles has walked out on Greece.
Tomorrow he sails home.'

'So I am right!'
'So I am right!'
In unison, Antenor and Anchises called.
And so again, as in that fountained square,
'True,' 'Shame,' 'Right,' 'Answer him,' and '. . . let her go,'
Became their dwindling differences, until
All were as quiet as children drawing.

Then Hector said:

'Listen to me, and take my words to heart.
This changes nothing.
I lift my hands to God,
Whose voice knows neither alien heart nor land.
He is my word, my honour, and my force.'
And went.

Immediately below the parapet
Of Troy's orbital Wall, wide, house-high terraces
Descend like steps until they mill

The flagstone circus ringing their Acropolis,
Whose acre top supports palace and palace walk,
Rooms by the flight where Priam's 50 sons
Slept safe beside their wives before Greece came.
    God's Temple faces south.
And over there notice the stairs that wind
Onto a balcony where Helen stands
And says:

    'They want to send me back.'

    And (taking a gel and pastry snail from a plate)
Paris replies:

    'Heaven sent you here. Let Heaven send you back.'

    And as they drive through Troy
Pandar assures Anchises' son: 'I never miss.
Artemis trained my eye. My future is assured.'
Achates looks aside.

    Go to the flat-topped rock's west side and see
Andromache touch Hector's shoulder:

    'Love,
I am a good and patient wife.
I speak the truth. My father was a king.
Yet when he slaughtered him
Achilles did not rubbish Etion's corpse,
But laced him in his plate and lifted him,
As tenderly I do our son, onto his pyre,
And let our 12-year-olds plant cypresses
Around his cairn before he burnt

Leafy Kilíkiax, its market and its wall,
And led them to his ships.
   Distrust cold words.
Friendship is yours, and openheartedness.
I hear your step – I smile behind my veil.
To measure you, to make your clothes,
Your armour, or to forge your blades,
Is privilege in Troy. You keep your word.
You fear disgrace above defeat. Shame before death.
And I have heard your bravery praised
As many times as I have dried my hands.
Be sure of it – as you are sure of me.
As both of us are sure
Courage can kill as well as cowardice,
Glorious warrior.'

   Then as they walk along the pergola
Towards the tower of the Skean Gate,
Shadowed by Rimph and Rimuna, her maids:

   'Half Troy is under 25, my love.
Half of the rest are wounded, widowed, old.
Hush . . .' raising her finger to his lips,
'Why else does Prince Aeneas take a boy
As young as Manto in his car?'

   'Aeneas is my business.'

   Silence.

   Then:

   'My lord, you never yet treated me like a she.
Do not start now.
   Your family quarrels are your own,' and walked

Before her skirts that trailed along the floor
Before him through the horseshoe arch
Into the tower's belvedere, retied
The threads of her veil at the back of her head,
Smiled Rimuna and Rimph away, then said:

    'Dearest, nearest soul I know,
You hesitate to fight below your strength.
Short work, therefore, to needle Hector with the thought
It was the tiredness of the Greeks and not his strength
That kept them out, that kept them down,
Or that he is too wise to face Achilles on his own
Out on the plain, far from the Wall.
But those who say so preach, not prove.

    Why, sir, even if you sent
Sarpedon, Gray, Anaxapart,
Back home to Lycia, Aeneas to his hills,
Prior to shouldering Agamemnon's race
Into the Dardanelles, alone,
Those propagandists would not change their tune.

    Day after day I wash Greek blood off you.
It teaches me that Greece is not exempt exhaustion.
    Send Helen back.
Let her establish a world-record price.
Desire will always be her side-effect.
And Achilleus is out.

    O love, there is a chance for peace.
Take it. We all die soon enough.'

    Hieee . . . Daughter of Etion,
From diadem past philtrum on to peeping shoes
You show another school of beauty.
    And while he looked
Over the Trojan plain towards the Fleet,

Your Hector said:
  'I know another way,'
And moonlight floods the open sky.

3

Now all creation slept
Except its Lord, the Shepherd of the Clouds,
Who lay beside His sister-wife
With Thetis on His mind.

So to a passing Dream He said:

'Go to the Fleet.
Enter its King.
Tell him this lie:
    "Strike now, and you will win.
God's lake-eyed queen has charmed the gods
And set a zero over Troy."'

Disguised as Nestor's voice, the Dream
Sank into Agamemnon's upside ear:

'Lord of the Shore, the Islands, and the Sea,
You know my voice. You know I speak the truth.
    You are God's King. He pities you. And is,
As always, on your side. These are His words:
    "War-weary as you are,
Strike now, hero and host, as one, and you will win.
My lake-eyed queen has charmed the gods
And set a zero over Troy."'

And as its host awakened, the Dream died.

Stentor to Agamemnon's tent.
Bright apricot rifts the far black.

He bows.

'Fetch my great lords.
Then have your less assemble Greece.'

And as his Stentor's lesser voices rang
From one end to the other of the bay,
Dawn stepped barefooted from her lover's bed
And shared her beauty with the gods,
Who are as then; and with ourselves, as now.

Outside.

Pylos and Salamis,
Crete, Argos, Sparta, Tiryns, Ithaca, and Macedon.

Formidable.

Even a god would pause.

But not himself.

'I have important news.
An hour ago,
Dressed in your voice, dear lord of Sandy Pylos,
God came to me and said:
"Make total war today, hero and host, as one,
Troy will be yours by dark."'

The dawn wind pats their hair.

Odysseus gazes at his big left toe.
His toe. Until Idomeneo said:

'Then you awoke, my Lord.'
'I did. And sent for you at once.'

A pause.

Then Nestor said:
'You say it had my voice?'
'It did.'
'My normal voice?'
'Your normal voice.'
'The voice that you hear now?'
'As now.'

Nobody speaks.

'Well?'

Nobody.

Along the beach-head's eastern reach
Stentor is assembling Ajax' men.

Then Diomed:

'My Lord, excuse my age.
Young as I am I wish to ask you if,
By "as one", by "total war", you mean us lords to fight
Beside the less?'

'I do.'

'My Lord, I am the child of kings.'

'And we are not?'

'My Lord, my uncle, Meleager, slew
The mammoth hog that devastated Calydon.
My father died while fighting for your own
Against the eyeless tyrant, Oedipus of Thebes,
And his incestine heirs. In Argolis
My family lands defend the frontiers of your own.
Perhaps the Queen of Heaven will offer me
A glorious death beneath the walls of Troy,
Or, if that is presumptuous, then at least
Wounds, without which no hero is complete,
A trumpet played into a drain.
    Of course you are delighted by the thought
Of taking Troy without Achilles,
And that our herd must fill the gap
That righteous lord has left.
    But, sir,
Why should I fight alongside my inferiors?
The herd is cowardly; a show of dirty hands;
Slop for Thersites' scrag; that have as gods
Some rotten nonsense from the East.
Bronze is for them to polish, not to wear.
Better be born a woman, leaky, liking to lose,
Or a decent horse, than one of them.
Bitter but better, fetch Peleus' son,
Tiptoe around him, pick one's moment, plead,
Than share our triumph with our trash.'

    A pause,
Then Nestor said:

    'Paramount Agamemnon,
Had anyone except yourself so dreamt
I would have begged him not to mention it.

But as things are, we will inspire
Both lords and less to fight for you.
Nine years is long. Hector is wise.
Unless we bring his army and himself
Out from the Wall, well . . .

As for yourself, young sir,
Remember that I fought beside your father.
He would say this:

What Heaven has ordered, Heaven can change.
If God says total war, total it is.'

See sheep in Spain: the royal flock
Taking five days to pass you as they wind
White from their winter pasture, up
Onto the Whitsun prairie of Castile
And wig its brow, then weed, with even pace,
That sunny height, meanwhile
Their collies chase the passing sky.

Muter than these
But with as irresistible a flow
The army left its lines and walked
Over the slipways, in between the keels,
Along the camp's main track beside the ditch,
And settled round the common sand.

All still.

Talthibios:

'Absolute silence for
Agamemnon of Mycenae, King of kings.'

'Fighters!' he said.
'Dressed in lord Nestor's words, our Lord and God,
Whose voice dethrones the hills,
Entered my head an hour before the dawn.
  These were His words:
  "Yours is the greatest army ever known.
Assault Troy now. Hero and host. As one.
And by this time tomorrow all its flesh
And all its fat will be your own to stow
As you prepare to sail for home; for I, your God,
As I have ever been, am on your side."'

  After nine years,
No throat that did not ache, then would not cheer,
Hearing such things.
  Yet as hope rose, so did Thersites,
And in his catchy whine said:

  'King,
God may be on your side, but if He is on mine
Why is Troy still standing over there?'
  Then capped our titter: 'How –
Us being the greatest army ever known,
Outnumbering Troy by three to two –
Have we not won the war?
  As for our sailing home,
Review the Fleet with me – but, O my Lord,
Please do not fart. You are a powerful man
And perished sails blow out. Then, when,
Us having scanned the shrouds, my Lord,
You stroke your chin and cast an expert eye,
Resist the urge to lean against a mast,
They are so rotten you can push a walking-stick
Clean through them.'

'True.'
'True.'

As he wades through our knees
Down to the front.

Will he step out?

He does.

He says:

'Son of Atreus, you astonish me.
You ask the Greeks to fight in a main vein for you,
Yet rob the man our victory depends on.
　What do you want?
More bronze? *More* shes? Your compound's full. And yet,'
Turning to us, 'who was the last man here to hear
Lord Agamemnon of Mycenae say: "Have this" –
Some plate – "brave fighter" or "share this"
A teenage she.
　One thing is sure,
That man would be surprised enough to jump
Down the eye-hole of his own knob.

　'Why laugh?
Achilles is not laughing.
The lords have let their King grab his mint she.
Achilles has been hurt. Achilles shows restraint.
If he did not' – back to the King – 'my Lord,
You would be dead.'

　Our shoulders rise and fall.
Something is going to happen. Soon.
　As from the middle sand Thersites shouts:

69

'Thick shes! – *I* have important news:
God is on Atreus' side, and on his captain's side.
    Comrades in arms with God, why,
Such lordies can take Troy alone,
Not share their triumph with their trash.
    So, timid nymphs, things to be stolen, tea
To his tablespoons, as he needs us
No more than our Achilles needs
Snot on his spearpole – we are free to go.
Go where? Go home,' and here some run to him
And raise his hands: 'By noon we can be rowing,
Seeing this hopeless coast fade,'
Hold his fists high, as:

    'Home . . .
    Home . . .
    Home . . .'

We answered him,
All standing now, beneath:

    'Home . . .
    Home . . .'

All darkened by that word,

    As sudden gusts
    Darken the surface of a lake; or passing clouds,
    A hill; or both, a field of standing corn,

    We flowed
Back through the ships, and lifted them;
Our dust, our tide; and lifted them; our tide;
Hulls dipping left; now right; our backs, our sea;
Our masts like flickering indicators now;

Knees high; 'Now lift . . .' knocked props; 'Now lift again . . .'
And our relief, our sky; our liberty;
As each enjoyed his favourite thoughts; his plans;
And to a Trojan watcher we appeared
Like a dinghy club, now moored on mud;
Now upright on bright water; and now gone.

So Greece near crowned its fate and came safe home,
Except the gods,
Whose presence can be felt,
For whom a thousand years are as a day,
Said: 'No.'

   Quicker than that,
At Hera's nod Athena stood beside Odysseus
And ran her finger down his spine.
   Aoi! – see him move,
Taking his second, Bombax, into their flight
Like flight; and saying: 'Wrap that dog,' hand
Bombax his crimson boat-cloak, and then leap
Onto a tilting deck and spread
His big bare feet, and cast
His landslide voice across the running beach.
   And she,
Teenaged Athena with the prussic eyes,
Split Ithaca's voice
Into as many parts as there were heads.
So each lord heard:

   'You are the best. You hold your ground.
You were born best. You know you are the best
Because you rule. Because you take, and keep,
Land for the mass. Where they can breed. And pray. And pay

You to defend them. You to see custom done.
What cannot be avoided, you endure.'

   So that mass heard
Odysseus' charming voice:
   'Be fair. The plague has gone.'
His wise:
   'Even if all Thersites says is true . . .'
His firm:
   'The lords are going to stay.'
His practical:
   'You know the sea?'
His hard:
   'Kakhead, get back into your place.'

   Hearing these things, the fighters slowed,
Looked at each other's faces, looked away,
Looked at the water, then about, and turned,
Re-turned, and turned again,
Chopping and changing as a cliff-stopped sea
Wallops, slapbacks its next, that slaps its next, that slaps.

   Bombax has got
Thersites in Odysseus' cloak
And roped it round.
And as he lumps it up the beach,
It starts; and those who watch it going by
Feel scared.

   There is a kind of ocean wave
Whose origin remains obscure.
Such waves are solitary, and appear
Just off the cliff-line of Antarctica

72

Lifting the ocean's face into the wind,
Moistening the wind that pulls, and pulls them on,
Until their height (as trees), their width
(As continents), pace that wind north for 7,000 miles.

And now we see one! – like a stranger coast
Faring towards our own, and taste its breath,
And watch it whale, then whiten, then decay:
Whose thunder makes our spirits leap.

Much like its suds the shamefaced Greeks returned
Along the many footpaths of the camp
And ringed the common sand.

Some minutes pass.

And then,
With his big, attractive belly rounded out,
And just a trace of dark grey hair
Ascending and descending to his cloth

Odysseus (small but big)

Half casually

Holding a broomstick cane

Strolled over to the still
Occasionally jerking item
Bombax had dropped onto the sand.

Then:
Stoop –
Grip –
And . . .

Hup!
Odysseus slewed Thersites out.
Who knelt.

  'Speak up,' Odysseus said.
'Think of your crowd.
As they brought you to life,
Because of you they see themselves
As worthy of respect. To have a voice.

  'No?

  'Not a word.

  'You must have something to complain about?'

No sound.

  'Then there, old soldier, I can be of help.'

  And raised the cane and gave Thersites' neck,
Nape, sides, back, butt, stroke after slow, accurate stroke,
And pain, lewd pain, a weeping pain, your smash-hit
High-reliability fast-forward pain. Took back his cloak.
Helped poor Thersites up, and said, softly to him,
But also to us all:

  'God *is* on Agamemnon's side.
Fear God – fear him. Fear him – fear me. Fear me –
And those like me – and save yourselves.
  As for Achilles: Sir,
That lord would sooner lose a hand than shake your own.
Let Panachea hear your voice again
And I will thrash you, bare, across the bay
From Ajax' to Achilles' ships – and back.'

That said, our shoulders parted
And Thersites sat
Touching his welts with one
And with the knuckles of his other hand
Wiping his tears away.

And as it is with fighters,
Shamed as we were a laugh or two went up:

'Baby on board!'
'Odysseus talks sense.'
'Shush . . . Shush . . .'

For having joined the greater lords,
And at Mycenae's nod taken the mace:

'Odysseus is going to speak.'

Some say the daylight sharpens where he stands
Because Athena guards him:

'So she does.'

And so we see her now,
Like an unnamed, intelligent assistant,
Standing a touch behind him, on the left.

Talthibios says:

'That those far off may hear
Full silence for
Prudent Odysseus, the lord of Ithaca.'

Who keeps his eyes well down,
Then turns his face towards Mycenae, saying:

'True King,
No Greek believes more firmly than myself
That all occasions are at God's command.
As God gave you, our King of kings, to us,
So you are given the best of all we take,
And you, through Heaven, ensure due custom done.

'Remember then' – turning his voice on us –
'You who believe the last thing that you heard;
Who tell yourselves you think, when you react;
Captains in camp, but cowards on the plain;
Keen to be off, but frightened of the sea –
You are not King. You never shall be King.
You see a hundred Agamemnons. God sees one,
And only one. Who bears the mace. Who speaks His word.
Who cares for us.
So keep your democratic nonsense to yourselves,
And when your betters speak to you – obey.

'At the same time, we veterans who recognised
Queen Hera's voice in Agamemnon's call,
Are sure Lord Agamemnon knows how hard it is
For anyone – lord, less – to be away from home,
Stuck on some island, say, no wife, no she,
Even for a month, let alone years.
But as we know this, so we know
The world has no time for a king whose fighters leave him.
Or would you have Obstropolous Thersites for your king?'

Swifts flit from spear to spear.

'Of course we are impatient.
That is Greek.

   'Yet, bad as it is
To be found drunk at sacrifice; worse
Not to hold your father in your arms;
To row with bowed heads home
Over the open graveyard of the sea
Then then walk empty handed through the door,
Must be the worst.

   'Those with the Fleet at Aulis will recall
King Agamemnon sacrificed his child,
Iphigeneia, plus 50 bulls,
For us to have flat seas and following winds.
And when their throats hung wide,
And we were kneeling by the smoky spring,
Beneath its cedar tree, before its stone,
A slug-white thigh-thick python slid
Out of the ferns that bibbed the stone,
Then glided through the lake of votive blood
And up into the tree and searched its leaves.
   Eight fledgling sparrows chirruped in those leaves.
And, as we watched, the python schlooped
Them and their mother up, tainting our sacrifice –
Or so we thought.

   'However, as the great snake fawned
And periscoped above the cedar's crown,
God stared into its eyes. And it was stone.
White stone. Figured with gold. Tall. Smooth white stone.
A thing of beauty from a loathsome thing.'

   'Indeed . . .'

'Then Calchas, full of fate'
(Sighting his finger on that seer),
'Opened those omens with these words . . .'
(Who swallows, stands, then recapitulates:)

'The time has come for Greece to praise its God.
What we have seen means this:
   Eight young – eight years before the Wall.
But when their mother's summer ninth has come,
Victory over Hector will be ours.'

'This is that summer,' lord Odysseus called
(Leaving the anxious Calchas on his feet).
   'To waste our King's dream is to scorn our dead.
So we strike now. Hero and host. As one.
Take Troy by total war. Then sail safe home.'

These were Odysseus' words.
And as he sat, Greece rose and roared:
   'Troy . . . Troy . . . Troy . . . Troy . . .'

Echoing in the hulls, along the dunes,
While Agamemnon stood;
Then, when they settled, sat. And said:

'I thank the Lord that Ithaca has found
The way to bring Greece to its senses –
And hope it manages to keep them.
   Similar silliness
Made me begin the quarrel with Achilles
About some foreign she.
   Well, well. God's ways are strange.
   This is the morning of the day
Whose dark will see Troy won.
   The lords will join me for the battle sacrifice.

78

The less will eat and arm.
    Never forget that we are born to kill.
We keep the bloodshed to the maximum.
    Be confident that I shall plant my spear
Deep in the back of any hero who mistakes
His shieldstrap for a safety belt; his feet
For running shoes. For soon, with God our Father's help,
Each one of you will have a Trojan she
To rape and rule, to sell or to exchange,
And Greece will be revenged for Helen's wrong.'

    And why, I cannot say, but as he sat
Our answering cheer was like the wave foreseen,
When, crest held high, it folds
And down cloud thunders up the shaken coast.

A hundred deep
The lords surround their lords:
    Merionez, Idomeneo's next,
His eyes the colour of smoked glass;
    Odysseus, unthanked – but unsurprised;
    Ajax (of course), and standing by him
Little Ajax – like a side of beef –
His brother by a purchased she;
    By him their cousin, Teucer;
    Diomed, short, slight, just 17;
    Thoal of Macedon, his hair like coconut,
Who always knows exactly what to do;
    And Menelaos, silent, doubtful, shy,
Watching lord Nestor lead a huge red hog
With gilded tusks into the ring,
Conscious his brother has supplied the sacrifice.

And all their world is bronze;
White bronze, lime-scoured bronze, glass bronze,
    As if,
Far out along some undiscovered beach
A timeless child, now swimming homewards out to sea,
Has left its quoit.

    Agamemnon dips his hands in holy water.
Talthibios, his barley scattered on the sand,
Snips a tuft from the hog's nape,
Waits for the breeze to nudge it off his palm
Into the fire. Then looks towards his King:

    Who prays:

    'Force Lord of Heaven,
    O Dark, Immortal Breath,
    Hold back the night until I break
    Into Hector's body with my spear,
    Fill Troy with fire,
    And give its sobbings to the wind.'

    'Paean . . .'
    'Vouchsafe us Troy.'

    Curls of high smoke
As if the air were water.
    The heroes kneel. Then lift their palms.
King Agamemnon draws his knife. Its point goes in.

    Ah me . . .
God took your hog but spiked your prayer.
Futureless spoons, God's name is everywhere,
God's name is everywhere. And when the barbecue
Of fat-wrapped thigh-cuts topped with lights,

And from its silver, sea-dark wine had crossed your lips,
Lord Nestor stood, and said:

'Today will be our longest day.' (But he was wrong.)
'The engineers will top the rampart with a palisade
Forty steps shipward from the ditch,
Which, while Thetis' son is not our front,
Will be our back.
   God stop that any lord,
Whatever place he holds, should die
Without hard fighting and renown.
   No more talk.
   The King will arm. You lords will join the host,
Answering our clear-voiced heralds as they call –
From mountain fastness, riverside, or lake,
Farm, forest, lido, hinterland, or shore,
Pasture or precinct, well or distant wall,
By father's name, or family name, or lord's –
The long-haired Greeks to battle, with this cry:

   "Lead on, brave King, as you have led before,
   And we shall follow."'

   Immediately
Wide-ruling Agamemnon's voices called
Greece to its feet, and set it on the move.
   And as they moved,
To stunt-hoop tambourines and trumpet drums,
The Daughter Prince, ash-eyed Athena, flew
Her father's awning, called the Aegis, blue,
Broad as an upright sky, a second sky
Over their shoulders' rippling estuary,
   And turned the pad
Of tassel-ankled feet, the scrape of chalk
On slate, of chariot hubs, back on itself,

And amplified that self; contained its light;
Doubled its light; then in that blinding trapped
Man behind man, banner behind raised banner,
My sand-scoured bronze, my pearl and tortoise gold,
And dear my God, the noise!
As if the hides from which 10,000 shields were made
Came back to life and bellowed all at once.
  See how the hairy crests fondle each other onwards as
From hill and valley, well and distant wall,
For the first time in ten long years, as one,
All those Queen Hera mobilised
Moved out, moved on, and fell in love with war again.

  'KING!' 'KING!'

  As shining in his wealth, toting the solar mace,
Thighs braced against his chariot's wishbone seatstays,
The Shepherd of the Host,
Lord of the Shore, the Islands, and their Sea,
God's Agamemnon in his bullion hat
Drove down their cheering front.

  'KING!' 'KING!'

20,000 spears at ninety, some
scaffolding poles, full-weight, to thrust,
        moving towards Troy; some light,
surveyor rods, to throw;
10,000 helmets – mouth hole, eye-hole
(like a turtle's skull), chin-strapped or strapless;
  'Move . . . Move . . .'
5,000 crests – T, fore-and-aft, forward curving
(though either will do), some half-moon war-horns;
  'Move . . .'
masks, nose-bars, some gold, some polished steel;

82

10,000 shields: posy, standard, waisted (and/or 'tower'),
two-to-six plyhide, some decked with bronze;
bows: single curve, lip-curved, lip-curved with reflex tip
(tested, found arrow-compatible);
    'Keep up, there . . .'
blades: short, long, leaf, stainless,
haft-rivets set square : : triangular ∴ with rat-tailed tangs
(these from Corfiot workshops, those imported);
    'Chariots!'
axes (single and double headed); slings (plus stones);
good (hay-fed) car-mares, each with her rug
(these double as body bags);
ships: long, black, swift, how many, how full;
400 tons of frozen chicken – their heads a world away;
a green undercoat;
and reaching the top of the swell in the plain:
    '*Now* see the Wall.'
barbs, barbs plus spur, spades, beaded quivers,
body-paint, paste flecked with mica, arm-rings,
chapati-wrapped olives, hemmed sheepskins
(in case it gets cold without warning)

    'KING!' 'KING!'

hear the high-pitched roar of armour advancing,
birth bronze, dust bronze, surgical bronze,
mirror bronze, cup bronze, dove
(seven parts copper to one part tin)
down the long slope towards Troy.

THE HUSBANDS

An Account of Books 3–4

'A drink! A toast! *To those who must die.*'

'On my land, before my sons,
Do you accept this womb, my daughter, Helen, as your wife?'
   'I do.'
   'Her young shall be your own?'
   'They shall.'
   'You will assume her gold?'
   'I will.'
   'Go. You are his. Obey him. And farewell.'

Troy.
   The Acropolis.
The morning light behind the Temple's colonnade.
Then through that colonnade, Hector of Troy,
Towards his mass of plate-faced warriors.
   And your heart leaps up at the sight of him,
And wonders of courage are secretly sworn,
As he says:

   'Torches and Towers of Troy, the Greeks are lost.
They dare not wait, but are ashamed to go
Home in their ships to their belovèd land
Without our city stowed. Therefore for them:
This desperate advance. Therefore for us:
Trumpets at sunrise from the mountain tops!
Our gods are out! Apollo! Aphrodite! so close,

You taste the air, you taste their breath, a loving breath
That shall inspire such violence in us,
Dear hearts, full hearts, strong hearts, courageous hearts,
Relaxing on our spears among their dead,
    "Heaven fought for us, 100 bulls to Heaven,"
Will be our pledge.
    I put my hands in yours.
Prepare to be in constant touch with death
Until the Lord our God crowns me with victory.'

    These were his words,
And knowing what you do you might have said: 'Poor fool . . .'
Oh, but a chilly mortal it would be
Whose heart did not beat faster in his breast
As Quibuph set the cloche-faced gull-winged gold
Helmet with vulture feather plumes on Hector's head,
And Hector's trumpeter, T'lesspiax,
Set the long instrument against his lips
And sent:
    'Reach for your oars!'
    'Reach for your oars!'
In silver out across the plain:
And then, as Hector shook his shoulders out, again,
Again, as Hector's throng gave a great shout of rage
As down from the Acropolis they flowed
And through the streets they pressed.

Breakfast in Heaven.
Ambrosia alba wreathed with whispering beads.
    'In the beginning there was no Beginning,
And in the end, no End,' sing the Nine to the Lord,
    As Hera's eyebrows posit: *'Now?'*
And now Athene goes.

Think of those fields of light that sometimes sheet
Low-tide sands, and of the panes of such a tide
When, carrying the sky, they start to flow
Everywhere, and then across themselves.
    Likewise the Greek bronze streaming out at speed,
Glinting among the orchards and the groves,
And then across the plain – dust, grass, no grass,
Its long low swells and falls – all warwear pearl,
Blue Heaven above, Mount Ida's snow behind, Troy in between.
    And what pleasure it was to be there! To be one of that host!
Greek, and as naked as God! naked as bride and groom!
Exulting for battle! lords shouting the beat out:
    'One –'
Keen for a kill:
    'Two – three'
As our glittering width and our masks that glittered
Came up the last low rise of the plain, onto the ridge, and

    'Now'

(As your heart skips a beat)

    'See the Wall.'

    And you do.

    It is immense.

    So high

    So still

    It fills your sight.

And not a soul to be seen, or a sound to be heard,
Except, as on our thousands silence fell,
The splash of Laomedon's sacred springs,
One hot, one cold, whose fountains rise or die
Within a still day's earshot of the Wall,
And in between whose ponds the Skean road
Runs downslope from the ridge, beneath the zigzags of God's oak,
Across the strip and up, until, under the Skean Gate,
It enters Troy, majestic on its eminence.

Within: Prince Hector's mass.
Without: a pause, until
Paramount Agamemnon, King of kings,
The Lord of Mainland and of Island Greece,
Autarch of Tiryns and Mycenae, looked
Now right, now left, along the ridge
Then at the Wall, then into Heaven, and drew his sword.
And as he drew, Greece drew.
And this dis-scabbarding was heard in Troy
Much like a shire-sized dust-sheet torn in half.
    A second pause. And then,
At Agamemnon's word the Greeks moved on
Down the long slope towards Troy
As silently as if they walked on wool.

    The gates swing up:
The Skean, the Dardanian, the South.

    Hector: 'Not yet.'

    'Not yet.'

    Then:

'Now.'

Think of the noise that fills the air
When autumn takes the Dnieper by the arm
And skein on skein of honking geese fly south
To give the stateless rains a miss.

So Hector's moon-horned, shouting dukes
Burst from the tunnels, down the counterslope,
And shout, shout, shout, smashed shouted shout
Backward and forth across the sky; while pace on pace
The Greeks descended from the ridge towards the strip
With blank, unyielding imperturbability.

100 yards between them.

50 . . .

Then,
As a beam before its source,
Hector sprang out and T'd his spear; halted his lines;
Then lowered it; and stood alone before the Greeks.

King Agamemnon calls:

'Silent and still for Hector of the soaring war-cry,
The irreplaceable Trojan.'

Then hands removed his shield, his spear,
And all Greece saw his massive frame, historical
In his own time, a giant on the sand. Who said:

'Greek King: I speak for Ilium.
We have not burned you in your ships.
You have not taken Troy. Ten years have passed.

Therefore I say that we declare a truce,
And, having sworn before the depths of Heaven to keep our word,
Here, on the strip, between our multitudes,
I will fight any one of you to death.

   And if I die' (this said within an inch of where he will)
'My corpse belongs to Troy and to Andromache;
My body-bronze to him who takes my life;
And to you all, Helen, your property, who was no prisoner,
       with her gold.

   And if I live: my victim's plate shall hang
Between the columns of Apollo's porch on our Acropolis,
But you may bear his body to the coast
And crown it with a shaft before you sail
Home in your ships to your belovèd land
With nothing more than what you brought to mine.

   Pick your best man. Commit yourselves to him.
Be sure that I am big enough to kill him,
And that I cannot wait to see him die.
Then in their turn, faring from world to world across our sea,
Passengers who come after us will remark:
"That shaft was raised for one as brave and strong
As any man who came to fight at Troy,
Saving its Prince, Hector,
Superb on earth until our earth grows cold,
Who slaughtered him." Now who will that Greek be?'

   Answer him, Greece!

   But Greece has lost its voice.

   Thoal is studying the sun-dried heads
And chariot chassis fastened to the Wall.

   Titters from Troy.

Then cannon off lord Menelaos': 'Me.'
'*No*. Hector will kill you,' from his brother.

Yet he has gone – how could he not? – out
Onto the strip. Alone.

But someone is already there.

Odysseus. The king of Ithaca.

History says,
Before Odysseus spoke he seemed to be,
Well . . . shy – shuffling his feet, eyes down – the usual things.
However, once it passed his teeth, his voice possessed
Two powers: to charm, to change –
Though if it were the change that made the charm
Or charm the change, no one was sure.

The sun gains strength.
Thoal has taken Menelaos' hand.

Odysseus:

'Continuing and comprehensive glory to you both,
Hector, the son of Priam, King of Troy,
Agamemnon, the son of Atreus, my King.
And to us all.

'I dare not speak for Heaven,
But as our Lord, the Shepherd of the Clouds,
Has honoured us by following our war,
Now, through Prince Hector's lips, He seems to say:
    Let the world flow through Priam's gates again
And Greece return to Greece with all debts paid.
    Lords of the earth,

93

We are God's own. Our law is His. Is force.
What better way to end this generous war
Than through the use of force – but force in small:
Not, all to die for one, but one for all.

The proverb says:
The host requires the guest to make himself at home.
The guest remembers he is not.
This is the reason why no Greek
Dared to pre-empt lord Menelaos' right
To take Prince Hector's challenge, even if –
Greece having sworn to keep the word it gives –
The Lord our God returns him to Oblivion.

Why wait, then?

Comrades in arms,
Hector has fought and fought, has given blood, and now –
Breathtaking grace – offers his armour and his life to end
The hostilities he did not cause.

Fighters! Brave souls! Surely that is enough?

So who should Menelaos fight . . . ? My friends,
Your silence says: Only fools state the obvious.
And as there's no fool like an old fool, so
It falls to me to state it:

'Paris.

'The handsome guest . . .'

'Yes.'

'. . . the one who started it . . .'

'Yes.' 'Yes.' (and rising)

'. . . among us on the slopes here . . .'

'Yes!'

'. . . who else to face the man whose property he stole,
Soft in his bed up there on the Acropolis?
Paris, with his undoubted stamina,
Will give our Greek a long and vicious fight to death . . .'

'Yes!'
'Yes!'

'. . . What fitter culmination to our war,
Or climax apter it to end?'

A beat, and then
The great assembly pleased itself with cheers
That bumped the Wall, and coasted on
Over the foothills and the moony dunes,
The woods and waterfalls of Ida, on –
Bearing their favourite thoughts and plans,
Their *'Peace for me'*, their joy at going home.

'Find him.'

At Hector's word,
Like dancers on a note, the shields divide,
And there, chatting among themselves, we see
Prince Paris' set; Pandar, his fan; Tecton,
The architect who built his fatal ships,
With Paris in their midst.

Napoleon's Murat had 50 hats
And 50 plumes each 50 inches high
And 50 uniforms and many more
Than 50 pots of facial mayonnaise
Appropriate to a man with tender skin;
He also had 10,000 cavalry,
Split-second timing, and contempt for death.

So Providence – had he been born
Later and lowlier – might well have cast Prince Paris.
    The centuries have not lied:
Observe the clotted blossom of his hair,
Frost white, frost bright – and beautifully cut;
Queen Aphrodité's favourite Ilian,
And though his hands are only archer's hands
(Half Hector's size), his weight half Hector's weight,
He is as tall as Hector (8 foot 9),
And as he walks towards him, note his eyes
As once his father's were: pure sapphire.

    They have not spoken for five years.

    'Oh, there you are.'
(Blowing a speck off his brother's plate.)
    'The world says yes to you before you ask.
I curse the day that you were born.
Your laughter pardons your betrayals in advance.
I see the hairnet dangling by your bed.
What does he do at dusk when other souls
Beg God to see them through the night?
The same thing that he does at dawn.
    Delicious sore –
It is a long time since you had the chance
To be the man you were the day you brought
Helen and Greece ashore at Ábydos –

Now burnt. Odysseus' work. Palookaville. Not worth the match.
Liagalia, burnt. Hac, burnt – to Troy,
Still standing. Just.
    Here is your chance to be that man again.
Take it, or I will strangle you with my bare hands,
Now, in front of Greece and Troy.'

Smoke from the morning sacrifice ascends.

    'Dear Ek, your voice is like an axe,' his brother said,
'My heart is weary with admiring you.
    How right you are. I brought the Greeks.
Still, if king Menelaos kills me, as he may,
Mind this: I take no credit for my beauty.
God gives to please Himself. If He is busy
Or asleep – one of His family may bless
A mortal soul, in my case Aphrodite.
I have been true to what she gave to me.
Not to have fallen in with Helen
Would have been free, original, and wrong.'
    He stands. So debonair!
    'Hail and farewell, dear Ek.'

Then to the lords:

    'See that the armies sit
With spears reversed and armour set aside.
    Then, he who had her first, and I, shall fight
On measured ground, between you, till
The weaker one, and so the wrong, lies dead.
    Thereafter, lawfully retained, or repossessed,
Let the survivor husband lead Helen of Troy,
And what was hers, away.
    As for yourselves: you shall, before we fight
Baptise your truce with sacrificial blood,

97

And pray that you may keep the word you give,
No matter who shall live. Then part,
Troy to its precincts and its provinces,
And Panachea in her troopships home
Across the sea to the belovèd land
Of Greece, of handsome wives.'

Eight o'clock sun. Some movement on the Wall.

They hated him. He was exceptionally beautiful.

Clouds.

Clouds.

Unanswerable magnificence.

'Hear me as well,' lord Menelaos says,
    'One person always comes off worst.
For ten years, me. Never mind that. Though Paris started it,
Everyone here has suffered for my sake.
But now that you have left the war to us
It does not matter which one dies,
Provided, when he has, you part
And ponder on it as you go your ways.
    One other thing. Though I have tried,
I cannot bring myself to trust Troy's young.
Therefore, old as he is, and ailing as he is,
I ask for *Priam*! Laomedon's son,
Great King of Troy, the Lord of Ilium,
To come down here onto the strip
With lambs – a black for Greece, a white for Troy.
Then, watched by us all, old Priam shall
Cut their young throats, and offer Heaven their blood,
For only he is King enough to make

Certain that Ilium keeps what Ilium gives,
And only he, the Lord of Holy Troy,
Adding his voice to ours, can turn those words
Into an oath so absolute
The Lord our God may bless it with His own.'

Agreed.

Now dark, now bright, now watch –
As aircrews watch tsunamis send
Ripples across the Iwo Jima Deep,
Or as a schoolgirl makes her velveteen
Go dark, go bright –

The armies as they strip, and lay their bronze
And let their horses cool their hooves
Along the opposing slopes.

Agreed.

But not in Heaven.

Queen Hera: 'Well?'
Athene:
   'They are about to swear and sacrifice.'
   'So . . .'
Touching the left-hand corner of her mouth:
   '. . . they do it frequently.' And now the right.
   'A common sacrifice.'
Glass down.
   'You mean, together? Greece and Troy? As one?'
   'As one.'
Settling her loose-bead bodice. Turning round:

'Who to?'
'To Him.'
'What for?'
'For peace.'
'*Peace* – after the way that Trojan treated us?'
'Peace, home, friendship, stuff like that.'
'It must be stopped.'
'At once.'
'It will.'

With faces like NO ENTRY signs they hurried through the clouds.

Snow on Mount Ida. Bearing king Menelaos' wish
Lord Thoal and Chylabborak's son, Kykeon, walk
Under the Skean terraces, and into Troy.

Troy. Less light. A sweetwood roof.
Sunshine through muslin. Six white feet.
Two sandalled and four bare.

They exit to the passages.

Troy. The atelier. Stitch-frames and large warp-weighted looms
    '. . . Paris is hated . . .'
Right-angled to the sills
    '. . . and so is she . . .'

The passages. Approaching feet. The women hesitate.
    'Ah . . . lady . . .' Soos (smiling) says and bows
Helen, her maids, on by.
    'I see young Nain has fainted.
Make sure he joins us on the terraces, Pagif.'

An inner court.
Gold loops across the sluiced coclackia.

    'All stand.'

    We do.

    She sits.
She lifts her veil.
She backs her needle out.
    'This is the only time she stops
Thinking of how she looks . . . .'

The terraces. Their awnings set since Dawn
Stepped dripping from the sea.
                    And up and in
Between the parapet, the flaps,
Murmuring shimmers drift.

    Soos:
    'Neomab has the plan, Pagif will check the seating,
Nain can watch. King Priam's brothers first. Pagif?'
    'On the back row –'
    'The *highest* row.'
    '– the fathers of King Priam's four full-brothers' wives;

Those brothers, and their wives; their brothers, and *their* wives.'
  'Excellent.'
  'Satraps of Thrace, of Bosphorus,
Marmarine Phrygiland and Hittite Anatolium Beyond . . .'

The atelier. On Helen's frame
  '. . . she will be fought for. In an hour . . .'
Achilles Reaches Troy, a five-year work
    . . .'To death?' . . .
Whose stitchwork shows that lord
    . . .'With spears.' . . .
Tall on the forepeak of a long dark ship
    . . .'Then they'll make peace.' . . .
  'Poo – Poo.' . . .
Dismantled chariots in its waist, who has
The kind of look that perfect health,
Astonishing, coordinated strength,
Pluperfect sight, magnificence at speed, a mind
Centred on battle, and a fearless heart
Display when found in congruence.
    . . .'What will she wear? . . .'
Observe his muscles as they move beneath his skin,
His fine, small-eared, investigative head,
His shoulders' bridge, the deep sweep of his back
Down which (plaited with Irish gold)
His never-cut redcurrant-coloured hair
Hangs in a glossy cable till its tuft
Brushes the combat-belt gripping his rump.
  What does it matter that he brought
Only 1,000 men in 20 ships?
For as they rowed their superchild between
The army's 30,000 upright oars,
  'Achil! Achil! The king,' the fighters cried,

102

'Whose Godsent violence will get us home!' so loud
The local gods complained to Heaven.

'Lady . . . my Lady . . . We must go,'
Cassandra, Priam's youngest girl, says as she lifts
The needle out of Helen's hand, who turns
Towards this serious 13-year-old wife –
As she once was – and lets herself be led
Across the dry-by-now coclackia, into stone.
  'There is a huge array . . . thousands of them!
And there's to be a final fight for you.
Not as per usual, though – blood everywhere.
They have calmed down, both theirs and ours,
All sitting quietly – their armour off, wheels parked,
You cannot see the foreslopes for its shine.
And round about the midday sacrifice,
Your two . . . I mean, my brother Paris and –'
  'Yes, yes.'
  'Will fight to death for you below the Wall.
But first you must be viewed. You are the property.
My father's satraps want to see the property.
It is their right. Please ask if I can watch.'

Cloud, like a baby's shawl.

  'How many names, Pagif?'
  '200 names.'
  'And stools?'
  '200 stools.'
Long rows of them. Silent and void. And suddenly

  All full!

Music . . .

An arch of bells,
A tree of china bells,
Two trees of jellyfish and cowslip bells,
All shaken soft, all shaken slow,
Backed by Egyptian clarinets.

   And they pass by.

   Then quadraphonic ox-horns hit their note,
And as it swims from slope to slope
Ten Trojan queens
Led by son-bearing Hecuba
Enter
And sit.

   A lull.

   And then,
And then again, but with a higher note, that note
Instantly answered by the snarl of silk
As Asia stands for Laomedon's son,
Priam of Troy, the Lord of Ilium,
His litter shouldered high, lord Raphno walking by its couch,
Onto the Skean terracing.

Helen, her maids – Cumin and Tu – wait   off.

Nothing will happen till he nods.

He nods.

The strip.
Chylabborak tumbles the lots.
Diomed takes one.
Paris's.
Paris will have first throw.

'We knew it was a fatal day,' Tu said,
'Long before Soos announced:
"Now see the beauty to be fought for with long spears"
And Nain said *Go*, and up we went,
The sweat was running down between my breasts.
But then we reached the top.   And lo!
The sun stood upright in the sky, and from beneath
The murmuring glitter of the slopes.'

What is that noise?

The fountains?

No, my friend – it is Creation, whistling . . .

All still.

100,000 faces tilt to her.
And fate, called love, possessed each one of them.
And each one caught their breath,
Parting their lips, stressing each syllable,
As one they breathed:

'Ou nem'me'sis . . .'

'Ou nem'me'sis . . .'

The boy who came from Corinth
Where the water is like wine:

'Ou nem'me'sis . . .'

This man from Abigozor on the Bosphorus.
And this unlucky nobody from Gla.

'At first, as we descended,' Cumin said,
'The silence held. But as she walked across
The level, leading to the lower flight,
One of our earth's great leaders gasped, and stood,
And then another stood, and then the rest,
Casting their gasps before her feet
As would the world its hats before a god.
   Of course, they were too old to fight,
But they were brilliant speakers.
Leaning together as they sat, they said:
   "You cannot blame the world for fighting over her."
   "There is no answer to a miracle."
   "But she must go –
If only for our wives' and children's sake."'

The strip.
Idomeneo carries round the winning lot.

'Sit here,' Soos said – between lord Raphno and the King,
Who spat into his bowl, then took her hand and said:
   'I had a wretched night.

You lose a husband. I may lose my eldest son.
Not that I blame you, child. You were Godsent.
Your people are incredible. Look there –'
   (Idomeneo)
   'Tell Raphno who he is.'
   She turns to him,
   'Once, though' – taking her back – 'I could have pushed you all
Into the sea with my bare hands, but now
The young know nothing about it.
   Feel this' – his thigh – 'lolly-stick wood.'
   Leaving her hand there, Helen says:
   'Of all the men I know
You are the only one I would call great,
Great, and still handsome, King of Fountained Troy.'
   Her voice is like a scent. To keep its prick
You must, as Raphno does, lean in.

   'I need forgiveness, too.
Not that I am the kind of she who calls the priest
Each time she has a cold.
I always wanted my marriage to be perfect.
To be his. Just his. As his is his.
And that is what my father wanted, too.
As did the world. And they are right. Quite right.
But then this thing. Your son.
I do not want to give that man a single thought.
He will not apologise. He says
A higher power gave me to him.'

   'It did, my child. It did.'

   'I was destroyed. The world turned upside down.
I have no saving touch of ugliness.
I trust almost nobody now. Hector, of course.

I know it would be better if I killed myself.
But all I do is cry. And that is so annoying.'

   She stands. She looks:

   'You see that Greek with the green umbrella?
That is lord Ajax, king of Salamis.
You like it when he comes into your room,
His big, broad face, his slightly bulging, slightly shyish eyes
Make you feel safe. A pious soul,
Concerned with the opinion of his fighters,
Not above asking them to pray for him.
And such a fighter! Even Achilles
Sees Ajax as the spear Greece counts on.
   Notice the lord just coming up to him.
He is an Islander, Nyro of Simi.
A distant relative of Agamemnon.
Well born, well bred, bearing a celebrated name,
No Greek – except Achilles – can match Nyro's looks.
The trouble with him is, he cannot fight
To save his own, let alone someone else's, life.
So though his father gave him three pine ships
No one would follow him to Troy
Until lord Ajax filled them.
   The man now carrying around the winner's lot
Is called Idomeneo, king of Crete.
Slack fighting niggles him. But though he lacks
The noble heart of my dear Menelaos,
My brothers say he has a valiant carelessness.
When all seems lost, there Ido is,
Grinning among the blades, inflicting big-lipped wounds,
Keeping his host's hearts high while thrusting them,
And holding them, against the enemy.

   'And now,' crossing to him, 'for you, lord Thoal.'

My how they stare. My how they wish that they were him.

'Like a white leopard,' Beauty said,
'The first thing that you sense in Thoal is,
Not strength, impressive though his is, but understanding.
    Lord Thoal knows that people love to have a side –
Taking a side as simply as a god.
And he himself would like to find a god
Who tapped his foot while humans danced.
He will get home. That is to say, regain his ilex-napped
Snowcragbackfastnesses of Macedon.
Ithaca is his uncle. His mother, Goo'io,
Was my belovèd mother's intimate. "Dear Goo'io,"
My mother said. "She was so douce. So funny."
The whole world wanted her to be its wife.
Lord Maha got her, though some said,
Beneath the trembling leaves of Mount Neritos –
What woman has not dreamt of it? –
God had her first.'
    The river Styxt flows east through Macedon,
And through the Styxt, but west, the Lethe flows.
So still their voice, so smooth their interface,
Lethe like oil, Styxt almost ice,
And through their reeds you glimpse no further shore.
    Her voice sinks back into her throat.
    'Sometimes I think I am in bed at home,
And as they did, my brothers come, and pull my covers off,
And I wake up to find that Troy is nothing but a dream.
Why are they not down there? Why have they never asked for
        me?
They hate the shame that I have brought on them.'
    But Troy was not a dream, and they lay dead,
Killed by their neighbours in a hillside war,
Beneath the snowy sheep that graze on Sparta.

Soos coughs.
Cumin and Tu lead her away.

Lord Thoal says:

'Favours from God to you, Priam of Asia,
And may the smile He uses to calm storms
Protect our truce.
    When wrong is done, one person always suffers most.
For Greece, lord Menelaos is that one.
He knows that Paris, your good-looking son,
Began, and has continued in this wrong.
He also knows that everyone,
Not least yourself, has suffered for it.
    Therefore, to make as sure as sure can be
That this day is the last day of our war,
Lord Menelaos asks that you, Great Sir,
Come down onto the strip and sacrifice with us,
For you alone are King enough to make
Certain that Ilium keeps what Ilium gives,
And can alone, as Lord of Holy Troy,
Promote that word into an oath, so absolute,
Our Father, God, may bless it with His voice.'

The windmills on the Wall are still.
King Priam stands. Then lifts his arms, and says:

'To sacrifice.'

And on the strip the drums begin to beat.

White horses on the sea, and on the shore,
Where the passing of the day is the only journey,

See
The first of the Immortals, known as God,
Strolling along the sand.

Poseidon surfaces.

'Good morning.'
'And to you.'

A pause. And then:

'Could I have Your opinion of the wall?'
'The wall?'
'The new, Greek wall.'
'You mean their palisade.'
'I mean their wall.'
'They have begun a palisade, but not a wall.
Walls, as you know, are made of stone,' God said,
As He resumed His steps.
'And as *you* know,' his brother said (wading along),
'We split the world in two.
You got the sky. I got the sea. And the earth –
Especially what the humans call the shore –
Was common ground. Correct?'
'Correct.'
'Then why is Greece allowed to build a wall
Across my favourite bay with nothing said?
Did I hear *aves?* No. Paeans? Not one.
Pfwah . . . do what you like with Lord Poseidon's honey sand,
No need to sacrifice a shrimp to *him.*
Just up she goes! Renowned as far as light can see!
The god – some seaside lizard sneezing in the weed.
His dignity – a rag. A common rag.'

'Brother,' God said, 'your altars smoke on every coast.
To catch your voice, grave saints in oilskins lean across the waves.
Try not to let the humans bother you –
My full associate in destiny. Between ourselves'
(Leading him out onto the sand) 'I may wind up this war.
And then, Pope of the Oceans, with Greece rowing home
You will have sacrifices up to here . . . and as they heave
Your train of overhanging crests can sink them pitilessly.
But later – when I give the nod.'

Hardly are those words out, when:

'Rubbish!'

They hear, and looking round they see
(Steadying her red-sepal hat with the russet-silk flutes)
Creamy-armed Hera with teenaged Athene
(Holding their scallop-edged parasol high)
As they wobble their way down the dunes,
Shouting:

'. . . truce . . .'
'. . . and an oath . . .'
'For peace . . .'
'. . . shameful peace.'
'In Your name . . .'

But as they near their voices fall,
And as they slow their eyes fall, too,
For looking into His when He is cross,
Is like running into searchlights turned full on.

'Imparadise Mount Ida, and,' God said,
'Tell Heaven to meet me there.'
And He was gone. And Lord Poseidon, gone

Backward into the depths,
His tower of bubbles reaching to the light.

Fierce chrome. Weapon-grade chrome
Trembling above the slopes.
And standing in it, leaning on their spears, among their wheels,
The enemies. And over all,
The city's altars, smoking.

A messenger runs along the strip.

Then nothing.

Then a boy selling water.

Then nothing.

Then nothing.

'Come on! Come *on!*'

Then 50 kings walk through

And greet –

Dressed in a silver-wool pelisse, his crown,
Of separate leaves, of separate shades of gold,
Each representing one of Ilium's trees,
As he is handed from his car –
Priam of Troy. Who says:

'King Agamemnon, from my Temple font
Accept this pyx of consecrated fire,'

(Which Soos holds out),
'Ilium's eternal promise to our Lord
That Troy shall keep the word it gives:
That when your brother, or my son, lies dead,
Our war will end.'

   'Ave!'

   That is:

   'Ave!'

   As Thoal slips
Into the line among the younger best
   'Ave!'
A lordly pace behind these lordly men
As they process between their multitudes
As they process, carrying the black lamb and the white,
King Agamemnon and Prince Hector, both,
Behind Dynastic Priam (8 foot 6; indigo skinned),
Correctly known as the Great King of Troy,
Himself behind a boy, who gives, each second step,
A rim-shot on his drum.

   In a plain bowl
Soos and Talthibios mix
Water and wine, and pour
Half of it over Hector's spear-arm hand:
   'Ave!' (but soft – some, trembling)
Then pour
   'Ave!' (so soft – some, weeping)
The half on Agamemnon's spear-arm hand.

   Then these are dried.

Then Hector took King Agamemnon's knife
(His feasting knife) and cropped a tuft
Of lovely, oily wool from each lamb's nape.
    And when these fingerfuls
(By Akafact for Troy, for Greece Antilochos)
Were taken to the overlords
And each retained a hair,
King Agamemnon said:

'Your terms are granted, Troy. Paris may have first throw.
But if he dies, as compensation for our long campaign,
We will require ten times the bodyweight
Of bronze, of tin, of silver, and of gold,
Of she the dukes must fight for, now, to death.'

It is the moment for the prayer.

'My son?'

Prince Hector prays:

'God of All Gods, Most Holy and Most High,
Imperial Lord of Earth, Sire of the Night,
And of the Rising Stars of Night, true King
Of waste and wall, and of our faithful selves,
We ask You from our hearts to let us end
Through one just death our memorable war.'

This was Prince Hector's prayer,
Tenderly, softly prayed.
    And as the silence that came after it
Increased the depth and wonder of the day,
The heroes filled their drinking cups with wine
Sainted with water, which is best, and sipped.
And what in them was noble, grew.

And truthfulness, with many meanings, spread
Over the slopes and through the leafy spears
As Priam thrust the knife into the white lamb's throat
(Which did not struggle very much) and pressed it down;
Into the black lamb's throat, and pressed it down,
Then, as the overlords spilt out their cups,
Lifted the pan of blood Talthibios had caught,
Bright red in silver to the sun
Between his withered arms.

   'Amen.'

   And then:

   – Two
          – Two
                  – Two-three

   The drum.

   'Amen . . .' (but stronger now) and now
The shin and bodice bronze of those about to fight –
   – 'Yes!' –
   – 'Yes!' –
Is carried up and down the strip.

   The lords:

   'We swear to kill, and then castrate, whoever breaks the oath.'

   And as the spears, the freshly gilded crests,
   – 'Yes!' –
   – 'Yes! –
Are carried up and down the strip,
The lords:

'Let both be brave, dear God. Dear God,
See that the one who caused this war shall die.'

Silence again. Then from the blue
A long low roll of thunder, of the kind
That bears fat drops. Though no drops came.
Finally, though, the sky stopped muttering, and then
From all:

'To You!'

'To You!'

Billowed into the light.

Here comes a hand

That banks

Topples through sunlit music
Into a smoothdownsideways roll

Then

Hovers above Ida imparadised

Salutes the gods, and

Out.

They smile. They are the gods.
They have all the time in the world.
What science knows, they know.

117

And Lord Apollo orchestrates their dance,
And Leto smiles to see her son, the son of God,
Playing his lyre among them, stepping high,
Hearing his Nine sing how the gods have everlasting joy
Feasting together, sleeping together,
Kind, colour, calendar no bar, time out of mind;
And how we humans suffer at their hands,
Childish believers, fooled by knowledge and by art,
Bound for Oblivion –
Until

   TRUMPETS!

   SUSTAINED!

   Sustained by sunlit chords:

   'High King of Heaven, Whose temple is the sky,'

Now the Nine sing, as,
Led by a flock of children through the dance,
God comes, loftly and calm, and lifts His hand.

   Then in the hush, but far and clear, all Heaven heard:

   'To You!'
   'To You!'

   'To You!'
   'To You!'

Midday. The measured ground.

In a fast slouch, the Trojan lord, the Greek,
Come on to it.
     Both men stand tall. Both men look large.
And though the Trojans hate him, they are proud of him,
Paris, his mirror bronze, his hair:
     'Be brave!'
     'He is more beautiful than God,' the children cry.
     But heroes are not frightened by appearances.
Under his breath lord Menelaos says:
     'I hate that man. I am going to kill that man.
I want to smash his face. I want to shout into his broken face:
You are dead. You are no longer in this world.'

The drum.

The 50 feet between them. Then:

'Begin.'

The Trojan turns.

Five steps.

Re-turns, and right arm back, runs –
     – Four – three – two
And airs his point for Menelaos' throat.

     But heroes are not worried by such sights.
Even as he admired the skill with which
Paris released his spear *'Dear God'* lord Menelaos prayed
'Stand by me' as he watched the bronze head lift
'Think of the oxen I' then level out *'have killed for You'*
And float towards his face. And only then

119

(As when, modelling a skirt, if childbride Helen asked:
'Yes?' he would cock his head) he cocked his head
And let the spear cruise by.
   And

   – 'Yes!' –

Cried the Greeks, but by that time
Their hero has done more than hurl his own, and

   – 'Yes!' –

He is running under it, as fast as it, and

   – 'Yes!' –

As the 18-inch head hits fair Paris' shield
And knocks him backwards through the air
(Bent like a gangster in his barber's chair)
Then thrusts on through that round
And pins it, plus his sword arm, to the sand,
The Greek is over him, sword high, and screaming:

   'Now you believe me! Now you understand me!'

Smashing the edge down *right, left, right,*
On either side of Paris' face, and:

   'That's the stuff! That's the stuff! Pretty to watch!'

Queen Hera and Athene shout, as Paris' mask
Goes *left*, goes *right*, and from the mass:

   'Off with his cock! Off with his cock!' *right-left,*

And on the Wall: God kill him (Helen to herself),
As Menelaos, happy now, raises his sword
To give the finishing stroke, and – cheering, cheering, cheering –
Down it comes: and shatters on lord Paris' mask.

  No problem!

A hundred of us pitch our swords to him . . .
Yet even as they flew, their blades
Changed into wings, their pommels into heads,
Their hilts to feathered chests, and what were swords
Were turned to doves, a swirl of doves,
And waltzing out of it, in oyster silk,
Running her tongue around her strawberry lips
While repositioning a spaghetti shoulder-strap,
The Queen of Love, Our Lady Aphrodite,
Touching the massive Greek aside with one
Pink fingertip, and with her other hand
Lifting lord Paris up, big as he was,
In his bronze bodice, heavy as he was,
Setting him on his feet, lacing his fingers with her own,
Then leading him, hidden in wings, away.

  Then both slopes looked this way and that and then around,
For there was no one who would hide that man.
And Menelaos is in torment, yes,
Is running naked up and down
Saying things like: 'Where did he go?'
'Somebody must have seen him go?' and then
He has gone down on both his knees, naked, on both his knees,
Shaking his fists at Heaven, and shouting out:

  'God God – Meek, Time-Free Trash,
Your hospitality is mocked.
And so are You. And so is Greece. And so am I.'

Athene comes to Him.

'Signor?'
'Chou-Chou . . . how nice . . .
Congratulations on your victory.'
    'I beg your pardon, Sir.'
    'A clear, decisive victory for your Greeks.
So that is that. Their champion she goes home,
The Sea can scrub that palisade, and peace can go the rounds.

    The armies wait.

    Picking a cotton from his sleeve: 'Pa-pa,' Athene said:
'This is not fairyland. The Trojans swore an oath
To which You put Your voice.'
    'I did not.'
    'Father, You did. All Heaven heard You. Ask the Sea.'
    'I definitely did not.'
    'Did-did-did-did – and no returns.'

    The armies wait.

    'Dearest Pa-pa, the oath said one should die.
The Trojan was about to die. He did not die.
Nobody died. Therefore the oath is dead.
Killed by a Trojan. Therefore Troy goes down.'

    Hector, Chylabborak, across the sand
Towards the Atreus brothers.

    'Father, You must act.
Side with the Trojans, Greece will say,
Were we fools to believe in His thunder?
Why serve a God who will not serve His own?'

And giving her a kiss, He said:

'Child, I am God,
Please do not bother me with practicalities.'

Hector and Agamemnon. Slope sees slope.

Drivers conducting underbody maintenance.

King Agamemnon says:

'Outstanding Prince, we live in miracles.
Our Lord and God, Whose voice dethrones the hills,
Has seen the beauty won.
    Let her first husband repossess her, and her all, and Greece
        obtain
Such previously unheard of compensation for its pain,
Those who remember us, will remember it
As long as they remember anything.
If not, I shall fill Troy with fire
And give its sobbings to the wind.'

Hector:

'Greek King, your brother, Menelaos,
Shall lead his wife, and that wife's gold, away.
And while she says goodbye, and Wall and slope
Wait while she walks across the strip into her husband's arms,
Let us, who fought for her together,
Make shade, and sit, and eat together,
Then listen to our story and shed tears
Together, for our dead, and for ourselves,
Among our horses and our hosts before we part,
You in your ships to your belovèd land,
We to our open city, or Beyond,

This afternoon, the favourable, on which,
In answer to my prayer, our peace began.'

Rain over Europe.
Queen Hera puts her hate-filled face around its fall,
And says to God:

'I want Troy dead.
Its swimming pools and cellars filled with limbs;
Its race, rotten beneath the rubble, oozing pus;
Even at noon the Dardanelles lit up;
All that is left a bloodstain by the sea.'
'Hold on . . .'
'No, no,' (wagging a finger in His face),
'I shall not stop. You shall not make me stop.
Troy asks for peace? Troy shall have peace. The peace of the dead.
Or You will have no peace until it does.'

The terraces.
Teethee, her granny-slave, calls Helen with her head.

'Athena?'

Sniff.

God sighs and says:

'Magnificas. You know how fond I am of Troy.
Its humans have believed in Me, and prayed to Me.
For centuries. If I agree to your destroying it,
And them, you must agree to My destroying any three
Greek cities of My choice – plus their inhabitants.
And when I do so, you, remembering Troy, will make no fuss.'

Their heads go close.

Below,
Cattle are being chosen for the sacrifice.

Athene: 'We accept.
Human for human, church for church,
Corinth and Sparta and Mycenae have
Believed in us, and so forth, for as long
As Priam and his ancestors in You.
Let us kill Troy, do what You like with them.'

'I can be comfortable with that,' He said.
And as they smiled: 'Except –
According to the latest estimates –
The total population of your three
Amounts to less than two-thirds of My one . . .'
    'Only,' Athena urged, 'if we include
Women and atheists, Pa-pa.' And Hera said:
    'Must we go into details?'
    'Ah, well,' God said. 'I like to please the family.
Have the Nine sing again.'
    'Dear Shepherd of the Clouds,' His sister said,
'I hate these quarrels just as much as You.
Send 'Thene to the strip, and while she finds
Some Ilian to get the war back on the boil,
You be the god who is a God to me.'

Cloud coral in deep seas. People with cameras.
Those sunlit chords.

'So, Prettyfingers,
Do as My wifely sister asks.' And she

Cast herself earthwards with a shriek of joy,
That echoed back as: 'I know just the man!'

Note Pandar's facts:
Sired by lord Kydap of the Hellespont,
Competitive, north Ilium's star archer,
He likes to chat, but has a problem keeping off himself.
And now, as Hector says: 'Make shade . . .' we centre him,
Practising bowpulls, running on the spot,
Surrounded by the shields he led to Troy,
                                        But O,
As Hector reached '. . . our peace began . . .' a gleam
(As when Bikini flashlit the Pacific)
Staggered the Ilian sky, and by its white
Each army saw the other's china face, and cried:
    'O please!'
(As California when tremors rise)
    'O please!'
As through it came a brighter, bluer light
Gliding, that then seemed like a pair of lips
Hovering, and then a kiss, a nursing kiss
On Pandar's wide-eyed mouth, who closed his lids
And sipped its breath and thus became
The dreaded teenaged god, Athene's, host.

Pandar has never felt so confident. So *right*.
Didanam, his old bow-slave, massages his neck.
    'De-de, I am a man.
Like day is light is how I am a man.
But am I man enough, I ask myself,
To put a shot through Menelaos' neck,

126

While he is out there waiting for his wife?'
    'He is our enemy. Our duty is to kill him, sir.'
    'And their cause with him, De-de. Think of that.'
    'Paris would give us a south tower, sir.'
    'Appropriate for a winning shot.'
    'A memorable shot.'
    Along the slopes
Horses are being watered. Fires lit.
    'However, De-de, one thing is against it.'
    'Sir?'
    'With their cause gone, the Greeks will sail,
So I shall lose my chance to kill Achilles.'
    'In that case, sir –'
    'No, De-de, Troy comes first.'
He stands.
    'I have decided. I will shoot him now.
Prepare the oriental bow and I will pray.'

The sweetwood roof.

    'Until I closed our doorbolt,' Cumin said,
'Old Teethee nattered about Paris' charm, his smile, etc.
Then all at once her squeaky words became
Spacious and clear.
    I sensed we were in trouble. Tu was green. At the same time
I wanted to be kissed and licked all over.
This is how Aphrodite sounds when she commands our flesh,
I told myself. And I was right. And we were lost. And then,
Twice in one day my lady was my lord . . .
    Putting her beautiful world-famous face
Down into Teethee's crumpled face, Greek Helen said:
    "I know your voice, lewd Queen. By using me
You aim to stymie lake-eyed Hera's spite." –

Talking poor Teethee backwards round the floor –
"So by some crossroad, or a lake, a cave,
Only this morning catwalked for the son
Of a Nyanzan cattle king whose Yes! to you
Has accessed him to me. Tu, Cumin – pack.
Make sure my pubic jewellery is on top.
Yours, too. God only knows whose threesome we shall be." –
Teethee now edging sideways down the wall. –

   "And all because the winner wants me back.
Lord Menelaos wants me back.
Oh yes he does. Oh yes he bloody does.
So your Judge Paris kisses me goodbye.

   Well, that's soon fixed.
As you and he have such a meaningful relationship,
Take my place. Of *course* you will give up your immortality:
Paradise dumped for love! Become a she –
How do I look? Will high heels help? And if,
If you try hard, your best, he may – note *may* –
Promote your exdivinity *Wife.* The apogee
Of standard amenities. No. That is wrong. I take that back.
Before the end of your productive life you bear
   'A boy?'
   'Unfortunately not . . .'
Why did you make me leave my land? My child?
Look at me. All of you. My head is full of pain.
Ih! – there it goes. Pepper my breasts.
Why should I go to Paris. I am lost."

   Those were her words. And as the last of them
Fell from her downcast face, Teethee reached up
And with her fingers closed those vivid lips.'

   Then in that handsome room, in Troy, it was
Just as it is for us when Solti's stick comes down
And a wall of singers hits their opening note
And the hair on the back of your neck stands up.

As she pulled Helen close, her form rose up
But not as Teethee's form, or as Miss Must
Wringing her hair out, wet. But as she is:
A god. As Aphrodité. Queen of Love. Her breasts
Alert and laden with desire in their own light,
Gloss of a newly-opened chestnut burr, her hair,
Her feet in sparkling clogs, her voice:
   'Do stop this nonsense, Helen, dear.
You are not lost. You never shall be lost.
You are my representative on earth.
You look around you – and you wait.
Try not to play the thankless bitch:
"Such a mistake to leave my land, my kiddywink . . ."
What stuff. Millions would give that lot
For half the looks that I have given you.
   You there: yes, you with the Egyptian eyes,
Prepare her bath. And you, Miss Quivering, strip her.'
   They do as they are told.
   'Turn round.'
Impartial as a sunbeam, her regard.
   'Your sweat, your wrinkle cream – quite useful. Eh?
Go through.' And as they did:
   'You wear a crown of hearts. Your duty is
To stir and charm the wonder of the world.
To raise the cry: *Beauty is so unfair!*'
Leaves. Tiles. The sky. 'And so it is.
Free. And unfair. And strong. A godlike thing.'
The water's net across the water's floor.
   'Be proud. You have brought harm. Tremendous boys
Of every age have slaughtered one another
Just for you!' Tu works the loofah down her spine.
'And as God knows no entertainment quite
So satisfying as war, your name has crossed His lips . . .'
(Now in a chair with one clog dangling.)
'Think of it, Elly – crossed His lips. And one fine day

129

The richest city in the world will burn for you,
Lie on its side and cry into the sand for you –
But, Sweetie, do not be too quick to leave.
After that business with the palisade
The Sea will see no Greek worth mentioning gets home.

'Dry her.'
We did.
'Oil her.'
We did.
'Dust her with gold.

'Come here.'
Tall, beautiful, alone,
Wearing a long, translucent, high-necked dress.
Gold beads the size of ant-heads separate her girdle's pearls.
'Bear this in mind:
Without my love, somewhere between the Greek and Trojan lines
A cloud of stones would turn your face to froth.
So, when they lift the curtains, and he looks – you hesitate.
And then you say: Take me, and I shall please you.'
Pause.
'What do you say?'
'Take me, and I shall please you.'
'Good. Now in you go.'

Lord Pandar prays:

'Dear Lord of Archers and Dear Lady Lord,
Bare-chested Artemis of Shots and Snares,
My blessings to you both
For blessing me with perfect sight
And for the opportunity to shoot

The Greek who caused this war,
A man scarce worthy to be killed
By me, your gifted worshipper.'

His bow-slave slips the bowstring's eye
Over the bow's iron ear, then plucks its string,
And hearing – as his owner stands – the proper note,
Hands him the bow, and bows. Then stands well back
Watching his blameless fameseeker assume
The best position for a vital shot.

   The shields divide. Lord Pandar's shoulder blades
Meet in the middle of his back; the arrow's nock
Is steady by his nostril and its head
Rests on the bosom of the bow.
Someone has passed a cup to Menelaos,
And, as his chin goes up, Troy's Pandar sights his throat,
Then frees the nock: and gently as the snow
Falls from an ilex leaf onto the snow
Athene left him, and the head moved out across the strip.

   But the god did not forget you, Menelaos!
Even as she left, Athene tipped the shot
Down, past your brother,
   – THOCK –
Into your pubic mound.

   Wait for the pain, wait for the pain, and here it comes,
Wham! Wham!

   '. . . aha . . .'

   Shield shade. Field surgery.
Odysseus, Ajax, Thoal, tears in their eyes.
Then Makon, Panachea's surgeon, saying: 'Shears.'

'. . . aha . . .' (but soft) and,
Opening the loincloth (fishline rolled in silver)
   There it is: in past its barbs,
A wooden needle resting in red wool, that Makon clips
   '. . . aha . . .'
   Then: 'This' (the vinegar) 'may sting.' And as it did,
Paramount Agamemnon, King of kings,
Sighed as he knelt beside you on the sand,
And all his lords sighed, too, and all his underlords
Sighed, and though they did not yet know why, the Greeks
All sighed as Makon cut, and Agamemnon said:
   'I love you, Menelaos. Do not die. Please do not die,'
(And cut) 'for you are all I have.
And if you die the Greeks will sail' (and cut)
'Leaving my honour and your wife behind.'
   Makon has nodded, and, as Jica kneels,
He and boy Aesculapius pull
      '. . . aha . . .'
The quadrilateral tabs of flesh his cuts have made
Back from the head for Jica's finger-strength to hold
Back and apart, while Aesculapius swabs,
And Makon looks, and Agamemnon says:
   'Oh, Menelaos. I have done so much for you,
Do not desert me now.
   You know what everyone will say.
He was a fool. When have the Trojans ever kept their word?
He should have done what they did – only first,'
   Makon sits back . . .
'And as the Fleet pulls out, the Trojans will parade her.
And her gold, along the beach.'
   The arrowhead has gone
Into the cartilage coupling the pubic arch . . .
'But nobody will blame Odysseus –
Although he organised the fight.' And looking up
His brother said:

'It may not be that bad.'

'It will be worse. I shall be treated like a strapless she.
Ignored. Pushed to one side.' His head is in his hands.

Now for the tricky part. As Jica parts the arch,
Makon will use his teeth/his neck to draw
The head out of the gristle by the stump.
His face goes down. He breathes. He bites. He signs.
And smoothly as a fighter-plane peels off
'. . . aha . . .' (my God, that man takes pain
As well as women do) lord Jica has the bones apart.
And sweetly as he drew his mother's milk
Makon has drawn the barbed thing out
And dropped it into Aesculapius' hand;
Who says (as he unlids the anaesthetic paste): 'Quite clean.'
Oh, stupid Pandar . . .

King Agamemnon stands.

His body shines. His face is terrible. His voice is like a cliff.
Taking a spear, and stepping, as his lords divide,
Out in between the slopes, he calls into the sky:

'Dear Lord, I know that You will not forget
The wine we poured, the lambs whose blood we shed,
And in Your own good time You will reduce
Truce-calling Troy, truce-spoiling Troy,
Oathmaking Troy, oathbreaking Troy, to dust.'

And now he takes a step, his lords behind,
Towards Hector, and he says:

'Bad Prince, God may take time. My time is now.
To shed your blood. To shed your dark red blood.
Your gleaming blood. And as you die
The last thing that you see will be my jeering face,

The last voice that you hear, my voice,
Confiding how my heroes served your wife
And kicked your toddler off the Wall.'

The terraces are empty.

The speaker turns
Back to his long bronze slope of men, and roars:

'There they are!'

'There they are!'

"The traitor race!'

'Let them die now!'

Troy. They lift the curtains. Paris looks.

'You sent for me?'
'You are my wife.'
'And his.'

'I have offended you.'

'Let's not burst into tears over that.'
'I owe you flowers.'
'A thousand white roses will do.'
'What then?'
'You go back down and fight for me again.'
She has not raised her eyes.
'It will be painless. He is fast – and heavy.'

'Tu.'
'My Lord?'
'My cloth.'

Naked. His curls
Bursting around his head like sunlit frost.
His eyes – so kind.

'Your death will be the best for everyone.
Troy will reopen. I shall sail for Greece.
And you will not survive your cowardice.'
'I –'

'"I am his better. I shall take his life" is what I heard,
So go back down and fight for me again.'

His shirt. His boots.
On.
On, and –

'Cumin.'
'Lady?'
'Retie my girdle.'

While she does:

'I have not finished.'
'Yes?'
'What happens if you kill each other?'
And through the lattice, in the pause – but far:

'NOW!'
'NOW!'

'Close it, Tu.'
'My Lord.'
'Leave it, Tu. I want to hear the strip.'
Shirt. Boots. All done.
'Well?'
He stands.
'If I had not said what I said you would have stayed,'
Turning away from him.

'NOW!'
'NOW!'

'Oh go then – you know what they say.
Up here: "The bitch will see us sold."
Down there: "Leave her to Heaven."'
He goes towards her back.
Cumin has closed the latticing, and now
She leads the others out.

'Beauty,' he says, 'I bless the day, the month, the year,
The season and the spirits of the place
Where we two met. Such heat!
But we were shivering with lust.
And when the crew had gone ashore to sacrifice,
Me, nude on the rug, you, little big girl,
Still with one thing on: "Shall I be naked, too?" you said,
And then: "Watch me get rid of it!" and threw it off,
And then yourself into my arms,
Into my arms, the world all gone,
And the sun rose early to see us.'
Leading her to the bed.
'The world will tell our story to itself.
And sit in silence to the end.'

Raise your binoculars.
The dukes of Troy – Hector among them.
Hector's face. Faces near Hector's face.
Aeneas, Akafact, Sarpedon, Gray, Anaxapart.
Faces near Hector's face say *Now*. Who says:
'When God says strike, we strike –'
  Swing to the Greeks,
See them helping each other on with their bronze.
  Aeneas: 'Now.'
Fastening each other's straps.
  Sarpedon: 'Now.'
'– But I will recognise that moment when it comes.'
  Yet *Now* has caught his slope. And now,
Quibuph, holding his vulture-plumed helmet,
Catches his eye. Then with his silver yard
Poised by his lips, T'lesspiax, his trumpeter,
Catches his eye. And then it is his next,
Chylabborak, adding his *Now* to theirs.
  But we are not in fairyland.
We know that it was not till God turned to His son,
The Lord of Light and Mice, and said:
  'Let Thetis have her way,'
That Hector, whose clear voice
Rose like an arrow through the trembling air,
Cried:
  'Hearts, full hearts, courageous hearts,
Our lives belong to God and Troy!' and waved them on.

  And when the armies met, they paused,
And then they swayed, and then they moved
Much like a forest making its way through a forest.
  And after ten years the war has scarcely begun,
And Apollo but breathes for the Greeks to be slung
(As shingle is onto a road by the sea)
Back down the dip, swell, dip of the plain.

And now it has passed us the sound of their war
Resembles the sound of Niagara
Heard from afar in the still of the night.

ALL DAY PERMANENT RED

An Account of Books 5–6

Slope. Strip. Slope.
Right. Centre. Left.
Road. Track. Cross.
Ridge. Plain. Sea.

Go back an hour.
See what the Mousegod saw.

Two slopes
Brilliantly lit
Double the width of Troy
Divided by a strip

30 yards wide.

The gentler, longer slope, that leads
Via its ridge onto the Trojan plain
Is occupied by 50,000 Greeks
Silent behind their masks, yearning to fight

But not until:

'Now!'
'Now!'

Hector emerges and commits the Ilian host
Their coffin-topped rhinoceros and oxhide shields
Packing the counter-slope

And presently the Skéan Gate is closed.

Out on the Panachéan right
Some cross-slope skirmishing.

The Trojan centre has begun to edge onto the strip.

The ridge.
King Agamemnon views Troy's skyline.

Windmills. Palms.

'It will be ours by dark.'

Not far from him, concerned
That in this final action those they lead
Should fight and fight and fight again,
The hero lords:

Nestor, his evening star.
His silent fortress, Ajax. Good – even on soft sand.
Odysseus (you know him), small but big.
Fourth – grizzled and hook-tap nosed – the king of Crete,
    Idomeneo, who:
    'Come on!'
Would sign a five-war-contract on the nod.

The Gate – still closed.

Across the strip
Lord Panda spots a Greek called Quist, and says:

'Watch this,' to his admirer Biblock as
He beckons up his oriental bow.

Then a shield hid Quist.

'Biblock, my father manufactures chariots.
I have a dozen. Lovely things.
I cannot bear to lose my horses in this war.
No mind. My motto is: *Start the day well.* An early kill.
It gets one in the mood.
    You know it was my shot that saved the war?'
    'I know it, Panda. Yes.'
    'However Biblock, mood, important though it is, is –'
Tapping his temple '– worthless minus brains.'

The armies hum
As power-station outflow cables do.
    The Trojan's edge.
The light goes upright through the sky.
    Downslope,
Child Diomed to those who follow him:

    'Still.'
    'Still.'

The King: 'I know Prince Hector. We will strike
When, as he always does, he stops to incite his host.'

Odysseus and Bombax have gone down
Slope-centre to their Ithacans.

The Trojans jeer: 'No fight!' and edge.

The Child:

'Still . . .'
'Still . . .'

'Biblock, my eyes are alpha.
But what your brain takes from your sight
Before it tells your biceps what to do, is key.
When the fighting starts you stick by me.
See brainwork work, not what the stars foretell.'
Which was, unluckily, what Biblock did.
    'Hold on, there is that Greek.'
And there was Quist.

To the sigh of the string, see Panda's shot float off;
To the slap of the string on the stave, float on
Over the strip for a beat, a beat; and then
Carry a tunnel the width of a lipstick through Quist's neck.

The Skéan Gate swings up.

Nothing will happen until Hector exits.

There is a touch of thunder in the west.

He does.

Odysseus: 'Thank God.'

Idomeneo: 'And about time, too.'

And, save for the edgers-on along the strip,
Prince Hector's thousands turn;
Then genuflect; then whisper:

'Now . . .'

'Now . . .'

'Now . . .'

Go close.

Besides his helmet and his loincloth Hector wore
A battle-skirt of silver mesh,
Its band, a needlepoint procession:
Sangárian tigers, each with a lifted paw.

The Gate swings down.

On either forearm as on either shin
Lightweight self-sprung wraparound guards
Decked with a slash of yellow chrome without
Dotted with silver knots and stars within.
And now –
As he moves through the light
Downwards along the counterslope, his shield,
Whose rim's ceramic fold will shatter bronze
Whose 16 alternating gold and silver radiants
Burst from an adamant medusa-Aphrodité boss
(Its hair bouffant with venomous eels
The pupils of its bullet-starred-glass eyes
Catching the sun) catching the sun,
Chylábborak, Aeneas and Anáxapart,
Quibuph, Kykéon, Akafáct and Palt
Cantering their chariots to the right of his,
His silver mittens up (a perfect fit,
They go with everything)

Sarpédon, Gray, Bárbarinth, Hágnet, Ábassee,
His favourite brother,
Cantering their chariots to his left:

'Still . . .'

'Still . . .'

Lutie, his nephew, this-day's driver ('fast and safe')
Catching his eye, flicking the horses on –
    On either side of him,
Beating their spears against their coffin-tops,
His army parts.

And now the Lord of Light filled Hector's voice
– Him moving on, on, forwards, down, towards the strip –
With certainty.
    And descant to his thousands:
    'Now!'
    'Now!'
    'Now!'
That full, clear voice, rose like an arrow through the air:

    'Are you ready to fight?'
    'We are!'
    'Are you happy to kill?'
    'We are!'
    'Are you willing to die?'
    'Yes!'
    'Yes!'
    'Then bind to me! I am your Prince!
In my command you will win fame!
The victory is God's!'

On hearing this,
To welcome Hector to his death
God sent a rolling thunderclap across the sky
The city and the sea
    And momentarily –
The breezes playing with the sunlit dust –
On either slope a silence fell.

    Think of a raked sky-wide Venetian blind.
    Add the receding traction of its slats
    Of its slats of its slats as a hand draws it up.
    Hear the Greek army getting to its feet:

    Then of a stadium when many boards are raised
    And many faces change to one vast face.
    So, where there were so many masks,
    Now one Greek mask glittered from strip to ridge.

    Already swift
Boy Lutie took Prince Hector's nod
And fired his whip that right and left
Signalled to Ilium's wheels to fire their own,
And to the Wall-wide nodding plumes of Trojan infantry –

    Flutes!
    Flutes!
Screeching above the grave percussion of their feet
Shouting how they will force the savage Greeks
Back up the slope over the ridge, downplain
And slaughter them beside their ships –

    Add the reverberation of their hooves: and
        'Reach for your oars . . .'
T'lespiax, his yard at 60°, sending it
Across the radiant air as Ilium swept

Onto the strip
Into the Greeks
Over the venue where
Two hours ago all present prayed for peace.
  And carried Greece
Back up the slope that leads
  Via its ridge
  Onto the windy plain.

Dispersed across its middle left
Extended lines of shields collide, totter apart
Shuffle back shouting in their ankle dust
Turning from lines to crescents, crescents to shorter lines
Backstepping into circles, or
Parties just wandering about aimlessly.

  And through their intervals,
Now moving, pausing now, now moving on,
His court – their comet's tail of wheel-dust – close behind,
Swift through the gorgeous light, Lutie on reins,
Lord of the Chariots, Hector's chariot goes
Racing across the left but seen
As the Mousegod wants him to be seen
As everywhere at once.

  Right now near Hyacinth the son of Hyacinth, a Greek
Able to quarry slate, throw a fair pot (and decorate it)
He chose to follow Agamemnon (still up-ridge
Still saying 'Ours by dark . . .') while Hyacinth stood
Alone in the dispersal, awed
By Hector's speed by Hector's light as Hector jumped
His sword – that caught the light – into his other hand

Leant out across the Troyside wheel
And wishing him the very best of luck
Decapitated Hyacinth as they passed
On, out, far left, U-turned beside Sarpédon, saying:
    'Dear Intrepidity,
Mark time until I tell T'lespiax to signal the advance.'
    Nodded to Gray, to Bárbarinth, told Palt –
The dearest of his court – to strip the headless Greek
And take his bronze-wear back to Troy
(Which Palt part did) then waved to them
As Lutie cracked his pair along the track that runs
Parallel to the strip, towards the middle of the slope.

G o there.

The situation is unpromising.

S panning the track
Some half-way up between the ridge/the strip
Fenced in behind their shields
2000 masks around Odysseus.
    Surrounding them lord Ábassee
With more.
    And over there
Coming down-track towards those roundabouts,
Hector and Lutie's dust.

    See Coriot and Shell
Ithacan hunters bred on Mount Neritos.
    Some said bare-chested Artemis
God of all animals bar us

Had taught these brothers how to ride and shoot.
She did not help them now.

  Running the horses off their chariot's shaft
They galloped, leapt the shields – and Bombax: 'No!' –
Knees in bows up straight at the coffin-tops
And never saw Lord Hector sign: 'Between . . .'
Or Lutie swerve off-track and put –
Now at full height gauging his cast, his shield
Sweeping Shell's bowshot wide – his Prince
Exactly where he asked. Who cast, and oh my God
As Hector's spear entered Shell's abdomen
The arrow's ricochet hit Coriot in the eye
And off he came, and died. As Shell,
Screaming, was bolted by his frightened horse
Into the Trojan coffin-tops
Where, axe up, Ábassee's minder, Dial, (with
The sound that a butcher's chopper makes
As it goes through a carcass into his block)
Finished him off.

  Long afterwards it was recalled
That Sheepgrove, Ithaca's adopted son,
Made sure that Shell and Coriot's parents got
The ashes of their twins, their only sons.
Therefore their high-roofed house
Above its wall of winding rock in distant Ithaca
Went to a farming aunt. While Palt,
Lost to the fame combat alone can bring,
Ignored (again) Hector's: 'Return the bodies of those two.'
Told Meep (his man) to see to it
And followed Hector back along the slope.

Headlock. Body slam. Hands that do not reach back. Low
    dust.
Stormed by Chylábborak, driven-in by Ábassee
The light above his circle hatched with spears
Odysseus to Sheepgrove:

'Get lord Idomeneo from the ridge.'

Then prays:

'Brainchild Athena, Holy Girl,
As one you made
As calm and cool as water in well,
I know that you have cares enough
Other than those of me and mine.
Yet, Daughter of God, without your help
We cannot last.'

Setting down her topaz saucer heaped with nectarine jelly
Emptying her blood-red mouth set in her ice-white face
Teenaged Athena jumped up and shrieked:
    'Kill! Kill for me!
Better to die than to live without killing!'

Who says prayer does no good?

Seeing Athena's cry raise fight and fire in lord Odysseus,
Hera, Heaven's creamy Queen, told Diomed
(Still near the strip, content amid the crackle of snapped spears):

'Odysseus needs you. Go.'

Beneath a rise
300 paces downslope from
Chylábborak and Ábassee
A party of 500 wandering Greeks
See Hector parked and praying:

'Lord of Light . . .'

While Lutie fills a bucket from the well
Where the Skéan road that runs from Troy
Straight up the slope to the ridge
Crosses the track.

'. . . I shall be busy until dark.
If I forget You, do not You, me.'

Out from the wanderers the Teucer boys
Iólo, 16, from a wife, and Párthenos
Bred from a she Teucer inherited
Come crouch-down hurrying convinced that this
Their chance for fame Prince Hector dead etc has come.
Párthenos set to plant his spear by Hector's spine,
Iólo, well . . .

Boy Lutie is astonished by their impudence
But not enough to not, in one,
Put down the bucket thrash his whip, its crack
Recalling Hector to his fate, its tip – as Párthenos
Jumped for the chariot's tailgate
And Hector's mittened hand snaffles his wispy beard –
Circling Iólo's wrist.

Párthenos kisses Hector's wrist.
His eyes are full of words.

'Take a deep breath before you speak, Greek boy.'

He does.

    'Please, Prince of the Gate, take us alive.
We did not want to come to Troy.
We could not disobey our father's words.
His mother was your aunt Hesíone.
He has a wall of swords –'
    'With silver hilts,' Ióto says –
'And gold – a chest of gold.
Please. Please. Please. Please.'

The wanderers edge in.

Hector steps down.
The Teucer boys may not have been the brightest on the slope
But they are bright enough to know death when they see it.
    'Keep your lives,' he said. 'A gift from Troy.'
And as they ran, made
    'Go' to Lutie with his head,
Studied the wanderers,
Lifted the bucket, doused himself
And charged.

    See an East African lion
    Nose tip to tail tuft ten, eleven feet
    Slouching towards you
    Swaying its head from side to side
    Doubling its pace, its gold-black mane
    That stretches down its belly to its groin
    Catching the sunlight as it hits
    Twice its own length a beat, then leaps
    Great forepaws high great claws disclosed
    The scarlet insides of its mouth

Parting a roar as loud as sail-sized flames
And lands, slam-scattering the herd.

'That is how Hector came on us.'

Despite the few who ran
Out from the rest to get at him and died
Or ducked and dodged his restless spear
And came away covered with blood and died,
Like shoppers trapped by a calamity
The rest pressed back onto the rest.
And he, partly to please his comet's tail,
Took sideway jumps – one foot up to the other in the air –
Chattering his spear along their front.

The ridge.

Sheepgrove (as asked).

Idomeneo does not wait.

Dustlight. Far off
A woman with an infant on her back
Is picking fruit.

Enter the Child.

Be advised,
If you cannot give death the two-finger-flip
Do not fight by or against Queen Hera's human
The son of Tydéus murderous Diomed aka the Child.

Tall. Blond. With a huge nose and lots of corkscrew curls.
Followed as he springs off his chariot's plate by 50 masks
And tells the wanderers
(As Séthynos, his heart, his next, springs down):
    'Your lord has come.'
Shoulders his way towards their front:
    'Honour him with your lives.'
Steps through:
    'Ave!'
Sees Hector far down front. Sees Palt
His custom chariot with Meep on reins
Arriving with the comet's tail.

    Palt was a kind, religious man,
Loving his Prince and loved by him.
Most days in pre-war days saw many guests
Around Palt's pool. But now, at 45,
Seeking the fame combat alone can bring
He chose to fight.
    Some said that God
Who recognises hospitality
Would save His worshipper – but no.

    As Palt and Meep tried to jump down,
Too far to stop it Hector saw the Child
Who did not break his stride
Or seem to notice them especially
Reverse his spear bash out Meep's eyes
Then re-reversing, plunge –
Mid-jump, with sword part drawn –
Its 18-inch bronze tooth
(That caught the light) into Palt's side:
And as premechanised harvesters their sheaves
Pitch him in dreadful pain sideways across his pair
Into the dust at Hector's feet.

Blind as the Cyclops with fraternal tears
Prince Hector prayed:

'God, stifle my grief,
And bless my plan –'

Which is:
To pull Odysseus' thousands (and now Diomed)
Onto himself, and hold them there, while signalling
The left and right wings of the slope
(Sarpédon's Lycians, Aeneas' Dardanelles)
To advance, turn inwards, meet, and so divide
The mid-slope from the ridgeline Greeks.

– Then stopped and put the Child between himself
And Palt, now on his hands and knees,
Holding the slick blue-greenish loops of his intestines up
Though some were dragging in the dust.
   Diomed telling Séthynos:
   'Finish him. Then strip that showcase plate.'
Taking a step towards Hector, who moved back
As Palt choked out:
   'Friend, I am gone.
I beg you not to leave the thing I was as dog-meat for the Greeks.'
   This
As Séthynos unlatched
And jerked his bloodsmeared urn off
While those behind the Child jeered:
   'Troy on a drip!'
As kind Palt died,
   And Hector, dogged by Diomed,
Hovered some paces off, hearing him shout,
Seeing his masks begin to butcher Palt:
   'Prince, by the light of Troy alight
Our herd will share what we Greek heroes left.'

'Yes!'
'Yes!'
'Who else can stop it if
Hector, the irreplaceable Trojan, lacks
The guts to guard the body of his friend?'

'Silence that liar with a single blow,' was Hector's thought
Though to Chylábborak and Ábassee he said:
'Fall back three spearcasts to the rise above the well.'

From time to time
Here on the agricultural
And poppy-dotted districts of the right-hand slope
Aeneas' thousands occupy, his lords
Lighting each other's pipes beside their wheels
Reckon the battle has as battles do
Found its own voice, that, presently far off
Blends with the sound of clear bright water as it falls
Over their covert's mossy heights;
A peaceful dust-free place circled by poplar trees,
Good cover and green shade.

Aeneas often sits apart.
He has his mother's face: white skin, green eyes,
A slow, unbroken look. And though there is
A touch too much of satisfaction in his confidence
As with the Prince your eyes incline to him.

'Ah . . .' standing '. . . Lutie.'

Sending for Panda and Achátes.

'Sire . . . . . . move when you hear T'lespiax' *Advance.'*
And he was gone.

Slope centre. Hear the Child
Shouting the shouts of an heroic lord:

'Strike for the face! The seat of the soul!'

Beseeching Hera as he ran
(That Queen so happy for herself and him):

'Blest Sister Wife of God
Give me the might and courage to become
The killer of the day.'

The masks behind him baying:
'Troy for us!'
Her power surging through him, he
Cast as he leapt at them; barbecued three;
Crashed through their coffin-tops;
Gaffed this plume dead; cut fillets out of those;
His masks behind him through the gap
Him making for the rise topped by Prince Hector's vulture plume.

Consider how, when sought,
The cliff-head whales that frequent
The sunlit radius of Antarctica
Tail down beneath its fields of rustling ice
Then 30 minutes later raise
Their rainbow spouts above a far lagoon.

So Hector trapped the Child, who made no mind
S-curving through these Trojans; hammering those;
As many arrows on his posy shield
As microphones on politicians' stands:

'I fight my heart out. Fight your heart out, Prince.'

Dust like dry ice around their feet
As Hector draws away
Onto and up the rise above the well, three spearcasts now
Above the Skéan Road
Beside him, Ábassee, Chylábborak, T'lespiax,
    Swish go their 18-inchers, swish,
Behind T'lespiax, Bóran, his instrumentalists,
Their silver-cuffed black oxhorns poised.

The Child is almost up to them:

'Front for a family of thieves!
No fouler being than a treacherous guest!'

His masks
Slipping and slithering up the bloodstained rise.
    'Who needs Achilles now?' calls Déckalin
(An eight-foot maceman from Arcadia)
Within a long jump of the Prince, who
Sweeping his spear detectorwise
Put Déckalin between the Child and himself,
Finessed his sweep into an upwards thrust:
    – 'Nice one!' –
That Déckalin (who saw himself – once home –
Beneath a tree, a drink in hand, describing Troy
Its wonders and its wealth) took on his noseguard's bridge.

Well manufactured as the helmet was
The spearpoint penetrated Déckalin's skull
And spurts of blood and bits of brain
Came through its tortoise holes.

And as the maceman's ghost stumped off,
Diomed:
    '. . . Yes . . .'
Watched for a chance to send the Prince
Gone Déckalin's body weighing down his spear
Into Oblivion
    'Yes . . .' as
Hooking his posy shield
Onto a finger of his spear-arm's hand
Hector signed:
    Advance to Boran and
    '. . . patience now . . .'
Raising their ox-horns to their lips
The trio sent a long deep even note
Over that dreadful world;
So otherwise it brought a pause; and in that pause
From either outskirt of the slope
The masses at its centre saw
Bronze beams tanning the dusty sky
And heard – the Child still eyeing Hector,
Hector still stuck with Déckalin on his spear –
Aeneas and Sarpédon's multitudes
    'Wait for it . . .'
Cheering far off as they advanced.
    'He is bound to show his throat . . .' Then
    'Yes!'
As Déckalin slid off,
As, Child, you took the breath to power your cast,
    He did
    And lord Idomeneo's fingers ringed your wrist
And lord Odysseus, thwarting Hector's plan, said –

'Who gives a toss what lord Odysseus said?' you said,
Offing the Cretan's grip:
    'Kill . . .' and aimed your spear '. . . my kill'
Hop-stumbling-forwards, watching it arc:
    'And I will you.'

Not your day, Dio, not your day.

    Jump from Aeneas' right
Hooves thundering in the dust
Cool-Heart-Boy-Lutie turned his bodice and his pair
Into the flight-path of your spear
Which pierced that urn
Then knocked him black back flat
Out of the car onto the sand
Further from Hector than from you
Longing to kill the Boy
Crying: 'Die! Die!' among the depth of cries
Idomeneo getting in your way,
Friendly – as we go tight – Odysseus':
    'King,
Come to the ridge.
Hector has pulled you, plus a third of us –'

– 'And I shall kill him as he pulls.' –

    Odysseus – that smile of his.

    And then, still far, yet louder now,
The outskirts' cheer, the outskirts' dust.

Sethynos says: 'Son of Tydéus, go or stay.
I am your next. If you die, I die. Choose.'

He hates to. He is loyal. They have gone.

And Hector's plan
(Albeit he got his Lutie back)
Is gone.

Host must fight host,
And to amuse the Lord our God
Man slaughter man.

The sea.
The city on its eminence.
The snow.
And where King Agamemnon drew his sword
And all Greece drew soon after seven today,
Flat, broad, declining stripwards, and
Double the width of Troy,
The ridge.

King Agamemnon sees Mount Ida's vines.
And that is all that he or Greece can see
Save for a coast of sunlit dust
Travelling upslope.

Miss Heber's Diary: 1908. Mid-June.
'We made our way through rain so thick
The midday light was as at home at dusk.
Then, suddenly, the downpour ceased, and there,
A thousand yards across, silent before our feet,
The great gold glittering Limpopo swept towards its Falls.'

So Greece saw Troy exit its dust.
But heroes are not frightened by appearances.
   'Ave!' we called.
'Our banners rising one by one
One after one accepting their advance.
Our kings delighting You
Dear Lord and Master of the Widespread Sky
With battle cries. Your cry:
   Strike now. As one. And you will win.

163

Our cry, as we, urns close, our masks like ripples on a lake,
Lowered our spearheads and prepared to fight.'

Troy silent. Slow. The dust
Wreathing up lazily behind their coffin-tops.

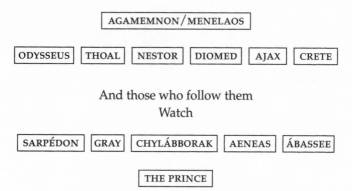

AGAMEMNON / MENELAOS

ODYSSEUS   THOAL   NESTOR   DIOMED   AJAX   CRETE

And those who follow them
Watch

SARPÉDON   GRAY   CHYLÁBBORAK   AENEAS   ÁBASSEE

THE PRINCE

This is the moment when you understand
That there is nothing in between
You and the enemy.
Too soon
You may be lying, one life less, seeing the past,
Or standing over someone you have known
Since childhood (or never known) beseeching you
To finish them,
Or on the run,
Or one of those who blindfold those who run,
Or one of those who learn to love it all.

THE PRINCE

(Glancing towards T'lespiax:)

'Forgotten kings
Put down your arms, run to your ships, launch them by dark

Or I will turn them into firewood.
And –'
And as he said so, Atreus, shouting:
'God for Greece!'
Floated the opening spear.

All in a moment on T'lespiax' note
10,000 javelins rose into the air
Catching the light but shadowing the ground
That lay between the enemies
    As Greece
Masks down, points down, in body-paint, in bronze
Beating their shields to trumpet drums and stunt-hoop
        tambourines
Advanced onto that ground
    While on T'lespiax' second note
Prince Hector's line of shield-fronts opened up
    – As Greece increased its pace –
To let their balaclavas led by Hux
(Who gave a farm the size of Texas for Cassandra)
Fender their scaffold pike-heads into Greece,
    As Greece:
    'Ave!'
    Now at a run
Came on through knee-deep dust beneath
Flight after flight from Teucer's up-ridge archers as:
    'Slope shields!'
    'Slope shields!'
The Trojan lords shout to their ranks,
And take the shock.

    Think of the moment when far from the land
    Molested by a mile-a-minute wind

The ocean starts to roll, then rear, then roar
Over itself in rank on rank of waves
Their sides so steep their smoky crests so high
300,000 plunging tons of aircraft carrier
Dare not sport its beam.
But Troy, afraid, yet more afraid
Lest any lord of theirs should notice any one of them
Flinching behind his mask
Has no alternative.
  Just as those waves
  Grown closer as they mount the continental shelf
  Lift into breakers scoop the blue and then
  Smother the glistening shingle
Such is the fury of the Greeks
That as the armies joined
No Trojan lord or less can hold his ground, and
  Hapless as plane-crash bodies tossed ashore
  Still belted in their seats
Are thrust down-slope.

Slip into the fighting.
Into a low-sky site crammed with huge men,
Half-naked men, brave, loyal, fit, slab-sided men,
Men who came face to face with gods, who spoke with gods,
Leaping onto each other like wolves
Screaming, kicking, slicing, hacking, ripping
Thumping their chests:
  'I am full of the god!'
Blubbering with terror as they beg for their lives:
  'Laid his trunk open from shoulder to hip –
Like a beauty-queen's sash.'
Falling falling
Top-slung steel chain-gates slumped onto concrete,

Pipko, Bluefisher, Chuckerbutty, Lox:
    'Left all he had to follow Greece.'
    'Left all he had to follow Troy.'
Clawing the ground calling out for their sons for revenge.

Go left along the ridge. Beneath,
Greek chariots at speed. Their upcurled dust.
    Go low along the battle's seam.
Its suddenly up-angled masks.
    Heading 2000 Greeks Thoal of Calydon
A spear in one a banner in his other hand
Has pinched Sarpédon's Lycians in a loop.

    Drop into it.
Noise so clamorous it sucks.
You rush your pressed-flower hackles out
To the perimeter.
    And here it comes:
That unpremeditated joy as you
– The Uzi shuddering warm against your hip
Happy in danger in a dangerous place
Yourself another self you found at Troy –
Squeeze nickel through that rush of Greekoid scum!
Oh wonderful, most wonderful, and then again more wonderful
A bond no word or lack of words can break,
Love above love!
    And here they come again the noble Greeks,
Ido, a spear in one a banner in his other hand
Your life at every instant up for –
Gone.
    And, candidly, who gives a toss?
Your heart beats strong. Your spirit grips.
King Richard calling for another horse (his fifth).

King Marshal Ney shattering his sabre on a cannon ball.
King Ivan Kursk, 22.30 hrs,
July 4th to 14th '43, 7000 tanks engaged,
'. . . he clambered up and pushed a stable-bolt
Into that Tiger-tank's red-hot-machine-gun's mouth
And bent the bastard up. Woweee!'
Where would we be if he had lost?

Back to today.
   At the loop's midpoint in the rising dust,
Continual drifts of arrowshafts and stones
Lessening their light, the kings of Lycia:
Sarpédon, Gray, Hágnet, Anáxapart
Silent and sorrowful.
   And queuing to that point lord Hágnet's followers
Raising their voices in farewell,
Each carrying, unasked, though under fire
The biggest stone that he can lift.
   'Oh, we have lost him,'
   'Oh, we have lost him,'
Then placing it
Onto the cairn those first in line have raised
Over their King, lord Hágnet's father, Bárbarinth
Who fell with honour where he fell seven times hit
Dust in his curls far from his home in Aphrodísias
Yet would not give a fingerslength of Hector's ridge to Greece
   Hector himself
Joining the queue adding his stone to theirs
   Taking Sarpédon's hand in his
Shouting above the noise:
   – 'When I have finished with the Greeks
Lord Hágnet shall have Crete.'

– 'Don't let me keep you, then.'
But he has gone, Lutie on reins across the battle's back.

Hay and manure, some pools of blood.
They look towards the centre of the ridge. Its dust, like trees.
   Aeneas says:
   'Delay. The day depends on you.'
   Hector: 'On God.'
   'Lock onto them. Exhaust them. Hope they charge.'

Oh, but they do!

The mid-ridge fighting is so intermixed
Its thousands heave, then rear, and then
Collapse back on themselves but cannot part.

   Hector is everywhere, the army king
Now moving pausing now now moving on,
The big bridge of his shoulders everywhere
His mittens flickering in the dusty light
His vulture plume the tallest plume the plume that says:
'Hector is here for anyone at anytime to find and fight to death.'
As he hacks his way on foot towards Chylábborak.

   Drums in the dust. Inside its mid-ridge overcast
Flags tossing above agitated forms.
   Chylábborak, holding the centre firm.
Blurred bronze. Blood? Blood like a car-wash.

Each time Greece drew its breath and smashed,
And smash they came and smash they came and smashed and
        smashed
Their eights into the line of coffin-tops,
Across the half-shield-high eye-tingling dust
Prince Hector's voice reached right reached left
And in them both both heart and voices raised
That reached and raised in turn Chylábborak's hearts.
Chylábborak calling:
    'Greece, is this the best that you can do?
Try harder, Greece.'

Oh, but they do!

Bow your head. Beg for your life. Death without burial.
And there – as if
    Inside a moonlit sandstorm God allowed
    The columns of Palmýra speech –
The Greeks encouraging their host:
    'I am here. I will help.
Stand still and fight. At any moment they will break.'
Though they do not.

    Chylábborak:
    'Greece, are you frightened?
Why come so far to die?' and unbelievably
Feeling the cobbles of the Skéan Road beneath his feet.
    And still –
    As one sits upright from a dream in which he drowned
    And reaches for the light –
Troy reached inside itself and found new strength,

Though Greece –
    Like a pedestrian who thinks: 'After this hill, downhill,'
    Then from its top sees yet another hill –
Kept coming back:
    'Yet some who looked our way would sigh for us.'

    Back from the dust, in quarter light
Masks up, bronze off, arms up, water dashed round
Happy to see each other through the dust,
Kykéon at his father's side,
Chylábborak shouts to Hector:
    'Even if I say so – which I do – our centre holds.'
A nod.
    'But it is not enough to lock/exhaust them.
They must be driven back.
And only you can make us do it.
Only you.'

    Kykéon smiles. He is Prince Hector's nephew. When
– As is the practice in South Ilium –
They estimate how long a boy's first spear should be
That year's cadets lie on their backs reach back an arm
And hope to lift the spear whose butt their fathers lay
Across their palms, in one smooth swing.
Kykéon (8) lifted a 10-foot spear, that Hector swapped
For his first (also ten) – its spearhead socket with a golden rim.

Impacted battle. Dust above a herd.
Hands wielding broken spearpoles rise through ice-hot twilight
        flecked with points.
    And where you end and where the dust begins
Or if it is the dust or men that move
And whether they are Greek or Trojan, well

Only this much is certain: when a lull comes – they do –
You hear the whole ridge coughing.

'There's Bubblegum!' 'He's out to make his name!'
'He's charging us!' 'He's prancing!' 'Get that leap!'
  THOCK! THOCK!
'He's in the air!' 'Bubblegum's in the air!' 'Above the dust!'
  'He's lying on the sunshine in the air!' 'Seeing the Wall!' 'The
    arrows keep him up!'
  THOCK! THOCK!
'Olé!' 'He's wiggling in the air!' 'They're having fun with him!'
'He's saying something!' 'Bubblegum's last words!'
'He's down!' 'He's in the dust!' 'Bubblegum's in the dust!'
'They're stripping him!' 'They're stripping Bubblegum!'
  'Close!'
  'Close!'
  'You can't see anything!'
  'His mother sold her doves to buy his plate!'
  'You can't see who to kill!'

Sunlight like lamplight.
Brown clouds of dust touch those brown clouds of dust already
      overhead.
And snuffling through the blood and filth-stained legs
Of those still-standing-thousands goes
Nasty, Thersites' little dog,
Now licking this, now tasting that.

Nestor, his son, Antilochus, standing beside him:

'Belovéd friends:
This stasis is God's work:
And it is blasphemous to win when He says wait . . .'

Hector is on his knees:

'Bringer of Daylight
Lord of Mice and Light
Help me to drive the Greeks
Into the sea.'

On Agamemnon's right, the Child,
Due to put on 10 years and lose 10lbs this afternoon:
    'We are Greek! We are brave! Add your strength to mine!'

As Lord Apollo answered Hector's prayer:

'Believer –
You are handsome, you are loved,
Bursting with hope and possibility,
Unyielding, ever-active, dangerous, true.
But no man can do everything alone.
    Speak out, speak up,
And I will help you drive the kings of Greece
Over the plain, across Scamánder, through the palisade
Into the shadow of their ships.'

'All souls!'
– You feel the god in Hector's voice –
'You are magnificent.
    Magnificent,
From Thrace, from Bosphorous, from Anatólium,
From Caran Lycia, from Phrýgiland,
Cyprus and Simi, Sámothrace and Cos,
    Magnificent,
My heroes and my host of Ilium.
    Now let us finish with the Greeks,

173

And drive them off this ridge that they pollute,
And chase them down the plain that they have scorched
And into the Scamánder they have soured.
And slaughter them beside their bloated ships.
   Founded by Heaven, founded in Heaven,
You of the never taken Gate to Asia, Holy Troy,
Rouse your brave hearts! Do as I do! Do as I say! Kill Greece!
The victory is God's! The victory –'
As with a downward sweep of his arm
Boy Lutie lashed their pair –
   'Is God's!'
And drove his Prince, his lord, his love, Hector of Troy,
T'lespiax trumpeting:
   'The victory –'
With 50 chariots on either side,
And running by their wheels, all answering his:
   'Is God's!'
   'Is God's!'
His mass
Followed him through the swathes of hanging dust.

Sparks from the bronze. Lit splinters from the poles.
'I am hit.'
'Take my arm.'
'I am dying.'
'Shake my hand.'
'Do not go.'
'Goodbye little fellow with the gloomy face.'
As Greece, as Troy, fought on and on.

   Or are they only asleep?
They are too tired to sleep.
The tears are falling from their eyes.

The noise they make while fighting is so loud
That what you see is like a silent film.
And as the dust converges over them
The ridge is as it is when darkness falls.

Silence and light.

The earth
And its attendant moon
(Neither of great importance
But beautiful and dignified)
Making their way around the sun.

  Bread trucks have begun to stream
across the vast plateau,
fair skies, high cumulus cloud –
the birds are in full throat
as the sun lights up the east.
  Who is it sees
Set in the north Aegean sea, their coasts
Nosegays of seaweed toasting Ida's snow,
The Isles of Imbros and of Sámothrace?
  And over there – grapes, ghosts and vocal grottoes –
Greece. Above it, Mácedon,
Its wooded folds declining till they meet
Those of Carpáthia at the Kágan Gorge,
Through which, fed by a hundred tributaries since
It crossed the northern instep of the Alps,
The Danube reappears.
  Eyes onto Italy
(Where squirrels go from coast to coast and never touch the
    ground)

Then up, over her cyclorama peaks
Whose snow became before the fire before the wheel, the Rhine,
Below whose estuaries beneath an endless sky,
Sand bars and sabre grass, salt flats and travelling dunes
Lead west, until, green in their shallow sea
That falls away into the Atlantic deeps
He sees the Islands of the West.
    He who? Why, God, of course.
Who sighs before He looks
Back to the ridge that is, save for a million footprints,
Empty now.

COLD CALLS

An Account of Books 7–9

Many believe in the stars.

Take Quinamid
The son of a Dardanian astrologer
Who disregarded what his father said
And came to Troy in a taxi.

Gone.

Odysseus to Greece:

'Hector has never fought this far from Troy.
We want him further out. Beyond King Ilus' tower.
So walk him to the centre of the plain and, having killed him,
Massacre the Trojans there.'

'Ave!'

Immediately beyond the ridge is Primrose Hill
Where Paris favoured Aphrodite.

'Take it,' said Hector.

Greece shouted: 'Hurry up!'
Troy shouted: 'Wait for us!'

Ｓee,
Far off,
Masts behind the half-built palisade.
    Then
Nearer yourselves
Scamánder's ford
From which the land ascends
Then merges with the centre of the plain –
The tower (a ruin) its highest point.

Ｈeaven.
Bad music.
Queen Hera is examining her gums.
Looking in through a window
Teenaged Athena, God's favourite child, says:
    'Trouble for Greece.'

    They leave.

Ｓea.
Sky.
The sunlit snow.

    Two armies on the plain.
    Hector, driven by Lutie,
    His godchild and his nephew,
    Going from lord to Trojan lord:

    'The ships by dark.'

The ruined tower.

In front of it –
Their banners rising one by one.
One after one, and then another one –
50,000 Greeks.

And on a rise in front of Greece
Two of its hero lords:

Ajax the Great of Salamis
Behind his shield –
As 50 Trojan shields
Topped with blue plumes, swivelling their points,
Come up the rise –
Lord Teucer (5 feet high and 5 feet wide)
Loading his bow,
Peering round Ajax' shield,
Dropping this Trojan plume or that,
Ordering his archers to lie flat,
Promising God as many sheep as there are sheep to count
If he can put a shaft through Hector's neck.

Prosperity!
Beneath the blue, between the sea, the snow, there Hector is
Surrendering the urn of one he has just killed
To one who thought that he had killed the same.

Lord Teucer's eye/Prince Hector's throat.
But God would not. The bowstring snaps.

Outside God's inner court.
The lake-eyed Queen, the Daughter, still in line.

The first so angry she can hardly speak.
    A voice:
    'The Wife, the Daughter.'
    'You go. His face will make me heave.'

God's court.
    Her blood-red mouth, her ice-white face:

    'Serene and Dignified Grandee.'
    'Papa to you.'

    'Papa' – His hand –
'I know you do not want the Holy Family visiting the plain.
But some of us would like to help the Greeks.
They lost their champion she.
Thousands of them have died. Now they are in retreat. Please
    look.'

    The plain.

    'You will come back the moment that I call?'
    'Of course, Papa.'
    'Then . . . yes. Encourage Greece.
But voices only.
Words. Shouts. That sort of thing. A move – and home you
    come.'
    'Of course, Papa.'

    The plain.

    Lord Teucer's archers hidden in its grass.

    Chylábborak, Lord Hector's brother-in-law, to his blue plumes:

'Move!'
'Move!'
And on their flanks, between the sea and snow,
Led by Teléspiax' silver yard
All Ilium's masks.

'Down came their points. Out came their battle cry.
And our cool Mr 5 × 5 called: "Up." And up we got
And sent our arrows into them,
That made them pirouette,
Topple back down the rise, leaving their dead
For some of us to strip, and some, the most,
To pause, to point, to plant, a third, a fourth
Volley into their naked backs. Pure joy!'

Chylábborak,
Holding his ground:
'Centre on me.
More die in broken than in standing ranks.
Apollo! Aphrodite! Our gods are out!
You taste the air, you taste their breath!
The Greek fleet, ours, by dark!'

Then he is ringed.

See an imperial pig harassed by dogs.
How, like a masterchef his crêpes,
He tosses them; then as they paddle back
Eviscerates, and flips them back again.
Likewise Chylábborak the Greeks who rushed.

Hector has seen it. As –
Beneath the blue, the miles of empty air,

Him just one glitter in that glittering mass –
The hosts begin to merge.

Fine dust clouds mixed with beams of light.
The Prince, down from his plate.
Either side's arrows winging by:
    'Cover my back.'
Finding a gap,
Dismissing blows as gales do slates,
Then at a run, leaping into the ring,
Taking Chylábborak's hand:
    'If you don't mind?'

Agamemnon:
    'Our time has come. God keeps his word.
Fight now as you have never fought.
We will be at Troy's gates by dusk,
Through them by dark,
By dawn, across our oars,
As we begin our journey home,
Watching the windmills on its Wall
Turn their sails in flames.'

Heaven. The Wife. The Daughter.

    Hands release black lacquer clasps inlaid with particles of
        gold.
Silk sheaths – with crashing waves and fishscales woven on a
        navy ground –

Flow on the pavement.

Hands take their hands

While other hands supply

Warwear,

Their car,

And put the reins into Athena's hands.

'. . . Troy's gates by dusk,
Through them by dark . . .'

The Hours, the undeniable,
Open the gates of Paradise.

Beyond

The wastes of space.

Before

The blue.

Below

Now near

The sea, the snow.

All time experts in hand-to-hand action –
Fricourt, Okinawa, Stalingrad West –
Could not believe the battle would gain.
But it did.

   Chylábborak's ring is ringed. And then no ring at all.
Some Trojans raise their hands in prayer;
Some Panachéans shout for joy and wait to drag the corpses off.
   Lutie, alone, the reins in one, his other hand
Hacking away the hands that grab his chariot's bodywork,
Rearing his horses, Starlight and Bertie, through,
   To,
   Yes,
   Chylábborak up; rescued;
Prince Hector covering. Then:

   'Zoo-born wolf! Front for a family of thieves!'
Lord Diomed, on foot, with Sethynos, his next.
   My Lutie answering:
   'Be proud, Prince Hector is your Fate.'
(Which will be so, though Lutie will not see it.)
   Chylábborak and Hector do not want to disappoint this oily
      pair:
   'Here come the Sisters Karamazov, Spark.'
Chylábborak said, 'Let's send them home in halves.'
And jumped back down.

Around the tower 1000 Greeks, 1000 Ilians; amid their swirl,
His green hair dressed in braids, each braid
Tipped with a little silver bell, note

Nyro of Simi – the handsomest of all the Greeks, save A.
   The trouble was, he had no fight. He dashed from fight to fight,
Struck a quick blow, then dashed straight out again.
Save that this time he caught,
As Prince Aenéas caught his breath,
That Prince's eye; who blocked his dash,
And as lord Panda waved and walked away,
Took his head off his spine with a backhand slice –
Beautiful stuff . . . straight from the blade . . .
   Still, as it was a special head,
Mowgag, Aenéas' minder –
Bright as a box of rocks, but musical –
Spiked it, then hoisted it, and twizzling the pole
Beneath the blue, the miles of empty air,
Marched to the chingaling of its tinklers,
A majorette, towards the Greeks, the tower.

A roar of wind across the battlefield.

A pause.

And then

   Scattering light,
The plain turned crystal where their glidepath stopped,
The Queen of Heaven shrills: 'Typhoid for Troy!'
And through poor Nyro's wobbling mouth
Athena yells:

   'Slew of assidious mediocrities!
Meek Greeks!
Hector will burn your ships to warm his soup!'

187

It is enough.

    Centre-plain wide,
Lit everywhere by rays of glorious light,
They rushed their standards into Ilium,
    Diomed (for once) swept forward;
Converting shame to exaltation with his cry:

    'Never – to Helen's gold without her self!
    Never – to Helen's self without her gold!'

    Mowgag well slain.
Hewn through his teeth, his jaw slashed off,
And Nyro's head beside him in the grass.

    When Nyro's mother heard of this
She shaved her head; she tore her frock; she went outside
Ripping her fingernails through her cheeks:
Then down her neck; her chest; her breasts;
And bleeding to her waist ran round the shops,
Sobbing:
    'God, kill Troy.
Console me with its death.
Revenge is all I have.
My boy was kind. He had his life to live.
I will not have the chance to dance in Hector's blood,
But let me hear some have before I die.'

    'I saw her running round.
    I took the photograph.
    It summed the situation up.
    He was her son.
    They put it out in colour. Right?
    My picture went around the world.'

Down the shaft of the shot in his short-staved bow
Lord Panda has been follow-spotting Diomed.

Between 'her self'/'her gold' he shoots.
It hits. And as its barbs protrude through Dio's back
Aenéas hears lord Panda shout:
    'He bleeds! The totem Greek! Right-shoulder-front!
How wise of Artemis to make
Panda her matador! Her numero uno! Moi!'

    Diomed hit,
The heart went out of those who followed him
And they fell back.

Shields all round

Diomed on his knees

Lifting his hands:

'Sister and wife of God'

As Sethynos breaks off the arrow-head

'Eliminate my pain.'

Settles his knee beneath his hero's shoulderblades

'Let me kill that oaf who claims my death'

Bridges his nape with one hand

'Before it comes with honour to my name.'

189

Then with his other hand
In one long strong slow pull
Drew the shank back, and out.

She heard his prayer.

Before their breathless eyes
His blood ran back into the pout the shank had left,
And to complete her miracle
Lord Diomed rose up between them, stood in the air,
Then hovered down onto his toes
Brimming with homicidal joy,
Imparting it to Greece.

Then Troy was driven back,
Trampling the half-stripped still-masked carcasses
Hatching the centre of the plain.

Aenéas/Panda.

'Get him.'

'*Get* him! I *got* him. *He is dead.* But there *he is.*'

And Diomed has spotted *them.*

'Calm down,' Aenéas said. 'Perhaps he is possessed.'

'What god would visit him?'

'So pray to yours – and try another shot.'

'Huntress,' lord Panda prays,
'Bright-ankled god of nets and lines,
Of tangled mountains and of dark cascades . . .'

But Artemis was bored with him
And let him rise, still praying hard,
Into the downflight of the javelin
Diomed aired at Prince Aenéas.

Sunlit, it went through Panda's lips, out through his neck,
     and then –
As he was swivelling into a run – through Biblock's neck.
And so they fell; the lord, face up; the friend, face down,
Gripping the blood-smeared barb between his teeth,
Between the sea and snow.

'It will be ours by dusk!'

Aenéas covers them.

Eyeing his plate
– Technology you can enjoy –
Diomed found, and threw, a stone
As heavy as a cabbage made of lead,
That hit, and split, Aenéas' hip.
Who went down on one knee
And put his shield hand on the grass
And with his other hand covered his eyes.
Dido might have become a grandmother
And Rome not had its day, except,
As Diomed came on to lop his top
Aenéas' mama, Aphrodité (dressed
In grey silk lounge pyjamas piped with gold
And snakeskin flip-flops) stepped
Between him and the Greek.

A glow came from her throat, and from her hair
A fragrance that betokened the divine.
Stooping, she kissed him better, as
Queen Hera whispered: 'Greek, cut that bitch.'
And, Diomed, you did; nicking Love's wrist.

Studying the ichor as
It seeped across her pulse into her palm
Our Lady of the Thong lifted her other hand,
Removed a baby cobra from her hair
And dropped it, Diomed, onto your neck,
And saw its bite release its bane into your blood.
    Then nobody could say
Who Diomed fought for, or for what he fought.

    Rapt through the mass
Now shouting at the sky, now stomping on the plain,
He killed and killed and killed, Greek, Trojan, Greek.
Lord/less, shame/fame, both gone; and gone
Loyalty nurtured in the face of death,
The duty of revenge, the right to kill,
To jeer, to strip, to gloat, to be the first
To rally but the last to run, all gone –
And gone, our Lady Aphrodité, giggling.

    While everywhere, my Diomed,

You beat your fellow Greeks
Back down the long incline that leads to the Scamánder's ford
Surely as when
Lit from the dark part of the sky by sudden beams,

A bitter wind
Detonates line by line of waves against the shore.

No mind. Even as Teucer backed away
He kept his eyes on you, hearing you roar:
    'You feel the stress? You feel the fear?
Behold your enemy Greece! the Prince God loves!'
    See Teucer's bow. Hear Teucer's: 'This time lucky.' His –
But this time it was not our Father, God,
Who saved your life, my Prince.
    As Agamemnon cried:
    'The ships are safe.
Stand at the riverside's far bank.'
Teléspiax heard the rustle of lord Teucer's shot
And stood between yourself and it.

His head was opened, egglike, at the back,
Mucked with thick blood, blood trickling from his mouth.
His last words were:
    'My Prince, your trumpeter has lost his breath.'

'Our worst fear was his face would fade,' Teléspiax' father said.
'But it did not. We will remember it until we die.'

'Give his instrument to Hogem,' Hector said, and went –
Lutie on reins – between the sea and snow,
Throwing his chariots wide, Scamánderwards,
As easily as others might a cloak.

Diomed in this traffic, on his own,
Among his dead,
Their pools of blood, their cut-off body-parts,

Their cut-off heads,
Ashamed as his head cleared
To see Odysseus, Idomeneo, the Ajax – Big and Small –
Whipping away downslope, you shouting at Odysseus:
    'Where are you going with your back to the battle?'
Who shouted back, although he did not turn:
    'Look left!'
And there was Lutie driving Hector onto him.

    Certainly they would trample him, for certainly
Queen Hera's human, Diomed,
Would stand and die, except:
    'Arms up, young king –' Nestor, full tilt,
Reins round his tummy, leaning out '– and
Jump . . .' wrists locked '. . . You young are just . . .'
Swinging him up onto the plate '. . . too much.'

    'With your permission, Da?'
Nod. Drew. Then threw the chariot's javelin
As Lutie spun his wheels, and Hector threw –
Those skewers trading brilliance as they passed –
And missed – both vehicles slither-straightening,
Regaining speed, close, close, then driven apart
By empty cars careering off the incline,
Or stationary cars, their horses cropping grass.

    'Daddy, go slow. Hector will say I ran.'
    'But not the widows you have made.'

    And slow
    And low
Cruising the blue above this mix
Heaven's Queen and Ringsight-eyed Athene
Trumpeting down huge clouds of sound
As Hector's car rereached king Nestor's, and:

'What kept you, Prince?' Diomed offered as they came
        abreast:
'You went for a refreshing towel?'
And threw his axe, that toppled through the air, and, oh,
Hector, my Hector, as you thought:
'If Heaven helps me Heaven shows it loves the best,'
Parted your Lutie's mesh and smashed into his heart.

What did you say as God called you to death,
Dear Lutie?

'My Prince, I leave you driverless.'

And put the reins into Hector's hands, and fled
Into oblivion

As Hector with his other hand
Held what his Lutie was, upright, face forwards, in between
The chariot's rail and himself,
Shouting as he drove after them:

'Loathsome Greek,
Your loathsome hair, your loathsome blood,
Your loathsome breath, your loathsome heart,
Jump in your loathsome ships,
I will come after you,
Come over the Aegean after you,
And find you though you hide inside
Your loathsome father's grave
And with my bare hands twist your loathsome head
Off your loathsome neck.'

There was a Greek called Themion.
Mad about armour. If not armour, cars.
Of course he went to Troy. And Troy

Saw a stray spear transfix him as he drove.
    Companionably, his horses galloped up
On Starlight's side, and muddled Starlight down,
And Bertie down, and brought the Prince
(Still holding Lutie) down, as all the world
Hurried, as if by windheads, on towards Scamánder's ford.

Whether you reach it from the palisade
Or through the trees that dot the incline's last stretch
You hear Scamánder's voice before you see
What one may talk across on quiet days,
Its rippling sunspangled breadth
Streaming across the bars of pebbly sand
That form its ford
– Though on the Fleet's side deeper, darkly bright.

  And here
Tiptoeing from this bar to that,
Settling the cloudy sunshine of her hair,
Her towel retained by nothing save herself,
The God of Tops and Thongs
Our Lady Aphrodité came,
Her eyes brimful with tears.

Scamánder is astonished by his luck.

'Beauty of Beauties, why are you weeping?'
'I have been hurt, Scamánder.'
'No . . .'
'Humiliated.'
'No.'
'Me. A god. Just like yourself. Touched . . .'
'Touched!'
'By a man.'
'A *man*!'
'A Greek.'

'Death to all Greeks!'
'He cut me!'
'Sacrilege!
 . . . But where?'
'I need your healing touch.'
'How can I help you if you do not show me where?'
'Moisten its lips and my wound will be healed.'
'You must say where!'
'Well . . .'
The towel has slipped an inch.
'I am afraid you will be disappointed.'
'Never.'
'Are you sure?'
'Yes!'
'You will not criticise me?'
'*No!*'
Her wrist upturned.
Out-turned.
Her opened palm.
Fanning the fingers of her other hand,
Stroking his spangles with her fingertips.
 'Goddess, I love you.
I have always loved you.
Say that you love me. Even a little.
I beg you. God grant it.'
 'I need your help, Scamánder.'
 'Take pity on me. Come into me.'
 'You have your nymphs.'
 'Bores! Bores!'
 'I might be nibbled by an eel!'
 'Death to all eels!'
The towel is down.
 'Step into me . . .
I love your toes . . . please let me kiss your toes . . .
Your little dinkum-inkum toes . . .'

198

'No one has kissed them so nicely, Scamánder.'
'And now your knees . . .'
'You tickle me . . .'
'And now your thighs!'
'Oh, oh, go on . . .'
'And now your bum!
Your Holy Bum! Your Sacred Bum!
The Bum of Paradise!'
'Oh, my Scamánder, I must have your help . . .'
'Anything!'
The towel goes curling off,
And as she floated on his stream
Our Lady Aphrodité said:
'At any moment now the Greeks will reach your Troy-side
bank . . .'

Recall those sequences
When horsemen ride out of the trees and down into a stream
Somewhere in Kansas or Missouri, say.
So – save they were thousands, mostly on foot – the Greeks
Into Scamánder's ford.

Coming downstream,
A smallish wave

That passes

But

Scamánder's flow does not relapse.

Indeed

Almost without a sound
Its murmuring radiance became
A dark, torrential surge
Clouded with boulders, crammed with trees, as clamorous as
    if it were a sea,
That lifted Greece, then pulled Greece down,
Cars gone, masks gone, gone under, reappearing, gone:

'Onto your knees! Praise Hector for this flood!
The Prince God loves!' Prince Hector claims
As he comes through the trees.

They do.
Then up and run, thousands of them,
To hold those Greeks
Under until their bubbles stopped; while those swept off
Turned somersaults amid Scamánder's undertow.

The flat –

1000 yards of it between the river and the palisade.

The King:

'The Lord has not abandoned us.
To cross will be as bad for them.'

But it was not to be as bad for them.

Indeed,
As Hector drove towards Scamánder's brink,

And as – their banners rising one by one,
One after one and then another one –
He and all Ilium began to enter it,
The river reassumed its softly-spoken, smooth, sunspangled way.

And Agamemnon cried:

'God, what are You for?
What use are You to me?'

As Hector cries:

'Two miracles!
Your Prince is close to God!'

And Hera to Athene:

'Fog?'

And fog came down.

And most of Greece got out.

Troy holding hands midstream.
An army peering through its masks

Miss Tops and Thongs to God:

'Your Hera has . . .'

And with a wish He turned the fog to light,

And with a word He called them back to Heaven.

Sky.
Snow.
The 1000 yards.
The palisade.

Hector:
'I am your Prince.
My name means He-Who-Holds.
Troy. And the plain. And now the ships.
    For Troy!'
His battle cry
Rising into a common cry, that cry
Into a clamour, and that clamour to
Bayings of hatred.

800 yards.

The Child:
'We are the Greeks. We fight to win. If one is lost,
Close his eyes, step over him, and kill his enemy.'

800 yards.

The Greeks are tiring.
Nestor is on his knees:

'God of all Gods, Most Holy and Most High,
If Greece has ever sacrificed fresh blood to you,
Protect our ships.'

Heaven.
Soft music. Summertime. Queen Hera and Athene? Yes . . .

    Some lesser gods
Observing their approach, approach,
Salaam, and then
Lead them –
Now both in black wraparound tops –
To God:

    'Darling Daddy, here we are.'
    'And' (Hera) 'here we stay
Until you stop that worthless Hector killing Greeks.'
    Up steps Love.
    Hera: 'Why is she wearing a tent?'
    Love: 'Father, see this.' (Her wrist.)
'Human strikes god! Communism! The end of everything!'

    'Darlings,' He said,
'You know that being a god means being blamed.
Do this – no good. Do that – the same. The answer is:
Avoid humanity.
    Remember – I am God.
I see the bigger picture.'

    'And I am Hera, Heaven's Queen,
Greece worships me.'

    'Stuff Greece,' Love said.
'Your blubber-bummed wife with her gobstopper nipples
Cannot stand Troy because Troy's Paris put her last
When we stripped off for him.
    As for the Ithacan boat-boy's undercurved preceptatrix,
She hates Troy because *my* statue stands on its acropolis.'

Hera: 'The cities' whores were taxed to pay for it.'
Love (Dropping onto her knees before Himself):
'Please . . . stop them harming Troy. The greatest city in the world.'

While Hera and Athene sang:

'Cleavage! Cleavage!
Queen of the Foaming Hole.
Mammoth or man or midge
She sucks from pole to pole.'

And God has had enough of it.

Lifting His scales He said:

'Hector will have his day of victory.'
Then crashed them to the ground.

7oo yards.

The palisade.

Its gate.

Late sunlight on gilt beaks.

'There's no escape from Troy.'
'Or from the plain at Troy.'

Begging for ransom, Trojan Hoti,
His arms around King Menelaos' knees.

King Agamemnon: 'Off.'

Then he punched Hoti in the face.
Then punched him in the face again.
And then again. And when he fell
King Agamemnon kicked him in the groin.
Kicking him in the groin with so much force
It took a step to follow up each kick.
Then pulled him up,
Then dragged him by his hair
This way and that,
Then left him, calling:
    'Finish him off.'
And someone did.

'I was 16. I said: "Where is Achilles?"
Hard as it is to share another's troubles when your own are
        pressing
Great Ajax took my hands in his and said:
"He loves us. He is with us. He will come."'

But he did not.

    Then Ajax to himself:
    'Dear Lord, you made me straight.
Give me the strength to last till dark.'

    The Prince: 'I get past everything I see.
Their war is lost.'

    It was.

    Aenéas, Ábassee, Sarpédon, Gray,
Calling to one another down the line.
    Then, with a mighty wall of sound,

205

As if a slope of stones
Rolled down into a lake of broken glass
We Trojans ran at them.

And now the light of evening has begun
To shawl across the plain:
Blue grey, gold grey, blue gold,
Translucent nothingnesses
Readying our space,
Within the deep, unchanging sea of space,
For Hesper's entrance, and the silver wrap.

   Covered with blood, mostly their own,
Loyal to death, reckoning to die
Odysseus, Ajax, Diomed,
Idomeneo, Nestor, Menelaos
And the King:

   'Do not die because others have died.'
   'Do not show them the palms of your hands.'

      'Achil!'
      'Achil!'
      'If he won't help us, Heaven help us.'

      'Stand still and *fight*.'
      'Feel shame in one another's eyes.'
      'I curse you, God. You are a liar, God.
Troy will be yours by dark – immortal lies.'
      'Home!'
      'Home!'
      'There's no such place.'
      'You can't launch burning ships.'

'More men survive if no one runs.'

But that is what Greece did.

Dropping their wounded,
Throwing down their dead,
Their shields, their spears, their swords,
They ran.

Leaving their heroes tattered, filthy, torn

And ran

And ran

Above their cries:

'I am the Prince! The victory is mine!'

Chylábborak:

'Do not take cowardice for granted.'

Scarce had he said it, when
His son, Kykéon, standing next to him
Took Ajax' final spear cast in his chest.

'I shall not wear your armour, Sir,' he said.
And died.

'My son is dead.'

The Prince:

'Hector is loved by God.'

And Greece, a wall of walking swords,
But walking backwards,
Leaving the plain in silence
And in tears.

Idomeneo,
Running back out at those Trojans who came too close:

'You know my name. Come look for me. And boy,
The day you do will be the day you die.'

Hector to Troy:
'Soldiers! –
Unmatched my force, unconquerable my will.
After ten years of days, in one long day
To be remembered for as many days
As there are days to come, this is my day,
Your Hector's day. Troy given back to Troy.
My day of victory!'
    And when the cheering died:
    'Some say: destroy Greece now. But I say no.
Out of your cars. Eat by your fires.
Two hundred fires! Around each fire
Five hundred men!
    'The sound of grindstones turning through the night,
The firelight that stands between our blades,
So let King Agamemnon's Own hold hands
And look into each other's frightened eyes.
    'True God! Great Master of the Widespread Sky!
If only You would turn
Me into a god,

As You, through me,
Tomorrow by their ships
Will see Greece die.'

.

Silence.

A ring of lights.

Within

Immaculate

In boat-cloaks lined with red

King Agamemnon's lords –

The depression of retreat,
The depression of returning to camp.

Him at the centre of their circle
Sobbing,
Shouting:

'We must run for it!'

Dark glasses in parked cars.

'King Agamemnon of Mycenae,
God called, God raised, God recognised,
You are a piece of shit,' Diomed said.

Silence again.

211

'Let us praise God,' lord Ajax said,
'That Hector stopped before he reached the ships.'

Silence again.

Then

Nestor
(Putting his knee back in):

'Paramount Agamemnon, King of kings,
Lord of the Shore, the Islands and the Sea
I shall begin, and end, with you.
   Greece needs good words. Like them or not, the credit will
      be yours.
Determined. Keen to fight, that is our Diomed –
As I should know. When just a boy of 10 I fought
Blowback of Missolonghi, a cannibal, drank blood,
He captured you, he buggered you, you never walked again.
But Diomed lacks experience.
   God has saved us, momentarily.
God loves Achilles.
You took, and you have kept, Achilles' riband she.'

   'I was a fool!'

   'And now you must appease him, Agamemnon.
Humble words. Hands shaken. Gifts.'

   The King – wiping his eyes:

   'As usual,
Pylos has said the only things worth hearing.
I was mad to take the she.

I shall pay fitting damages.
Plus her, I offer him
The Corfiot armour that my father wore.'

Silence.

The sea.

Its whispering.

'To which I add: a set of shields.
Posy, standard, ceremonial.
The last, cut from the hide of a one ton Lesbian bull.'

Silence.

The sea.

'And . . . a chariot!
From my own équipe!
They smoke along the ground . . .
They ride its undulations like a breeze . . .'

The sea.

'Plus: six horses – saddled, bridled and caparisoned,
Their grooms and veterinarians . . .

'. . . And six tall shes:
Two good dancers, two good stitchers, two good cooks.
All capable of bearing boys . . .

'Oh, very well then: twenty loaves of gold,
The same of silver, and the same of iron.'

Masks. Lights.
Behind the lords
Some hundreds from the army have walked up.

Lord Nestor smiles.
Lord Menelaos smiles.

'Plus –
Though it may well reduce your King to destitution:
   A'kimi'kúriex,
My summer palace by the Argive sea,
Its lawns, its terraces, its curtains in whose depths
Larks dive above a field of waving lilies
And fishscale-breakers shatter on blue rocks.
Then, as he draws their silky heights aside,
Standing among huge chests of looted booty,
Long necked, with lowered lids, but candid eyes,
My living daughter, Íphaniss, a diamond
Big as a cheeseball for her belly stud.
His wife to be! minus – I need not say – her otherwise huge
   bride-price.'

'More!'
'More!'
'More!'

Lord Ajax almost has to hold him up.

'The whole of eastern Pel'po'nesia –
An area of outstanding natural beauty –
Its cities, Epi'dávros, Trów'é'zen,
Their fortresses, their harbours and their fleets,
Their taxpayers – glad to accept his modest ways –
All this, the greatest benefaction ever known,
If he agrees to fight. And he admits I am his King.'

Instantly, Nestor:

'An offer God himself could not refuse.
All that remains to say is:
Who shall take it to Achilles?'

Agamemnon: 'You will.'

Starlight.

The starlight on the sea.

The sea.

Its whispering

Mixed with the prayers
Of Ajax and of Nestor as they walk
Along the shore towards Achilles' gate.

'My lords?'

'Your lord.'

'This way.'

They find him, with guitar,
Singing of Gilgamesh.

  'Take my hands. Here they are.'

  You cannot take your eyes away from him.
His own so bright they slow you down.
His voice so low, and yet so clear.
You know that he is dangerous.

  'Patroclus?
Friends in need.
  Still,
Friends.
  That has not changed,
I think.
  Autómedon? Wine.'

  '*Dear Lord and Master of the Widespread Sky,*
Accept ourselves, accept our prayers.'

Their cups are taken.

'Father friend?'

King Nestor (for his life):

'You know why we are here.
  We face death.

The mass choose slavery.
Mycenae has admitted he was wrong to wrong yourself.
In recompense he offers you
The greatest benefaction ever known.
Take it, and fight. Otherwise Hector will ignite the ships
Then kill us randomly.

Remember what your Father said
The day when Ajax and myself drove up to ask
If you could come with us to Troy?
That you should stand among the blades where honour grows.
And secondly, to let your anger go.

Spirit, and strength, and beauty have combined
Such awesome power in you
A vacant Heaven would offer you its throne.
Think of what those who will come after us will say.

Save us from Hector's god, from Hector, and from Hector's
force.
I go down on my knees to you, Achilles.'

'. . . Please . . . No bullying.
Indeed, it is a while since we spoke.'

A pause.

'I must admire your courage, father friend,
For treating me as if I was a fool.
I shall deal with Hector as I want to.
You and your fellow countrymen will die
For how your king has treated me.

'I have spent five years fighting for your King.
My record is: 10 coastal and 10 inland cities
Burnt to the ground. Their males, massacred.
Their cattle, and their women, given to him.
Among the rest, Briseis the Beautiful, my riband she.

217

Not that I got her courtesy of him.
She joined my stock in recognition of
My strength, my courage, my superiority.
Courtesy of yourselves, my lords.
    I will not fight for him.
He aims to personalise my loss.
Briseis taken from Achilles – standard practice:
Helen from Menelaos – war.
    Lord Busy Busy, building his palisade, mounting my she,
One that I might have picked to run my house,
Raising her to the status of a wife.
    Do I hate him? Yes, I hate him. Hate him.
And should he be afraid of me? He should.
I want to harm him. I want him to feel pain.
In his body, and between his ears.
    I must admit,
Some of the things that you have said are true.
But look what he has done to me! To *me*!
The king on whom his kingliness depends!
I will not fight for him.
    Hearing your steps, I thought: at last,
My friends have come to visit me.
They took their time about it, true –
After he took my she none of you came –
Now, though – admittedly they are in trouble,
Serious trouble – they have arrived as friends,
And of their own accord.
    But you have not come here as friends.
And you have not come of your own accord.
You came because your king told you to come.
You came because I am his last resort.
And, incidentally, your last resort.

    'At least he offers stuff.
All you have offered is advice:

218

"Keep your temper . . .
Mind your tongue . . .
Think what the world will say . . ."
No mention of your king's treatment of me.
No sign of love for me behind your tears.
    I will not fight for him.
    I can remember very well indeed
The day you two grand lords came visiting my father's house,
How I ran out to you, and took your hands –
The greatest men that I had ever seen:
Ajax, my fighting cousin, strong, brave, unafraid to die;
Nestor, the King of Sandy Pylos, wisdom's sword.
And then, when all had had enough to eat and drink
And it was sealed that I should come to Troy,
Then my dear father said that lordship knows
Not only how to fight, and when to hold its tongue,
But of the difference between a child enraged
And honour-bound lords.
    I will not fight for him.
    There is a King to be maintained. You are his lords.
My fighting powers prove my inferiority.
Whatever he, through you, may grant,
I must receive it as a favour, not of right,
Go back to him with downcast looks, a suppliant tone,
Acknowledge my transgressions – I did not
Applaud his sticky fingers on my she's meek flesh.
    My mother says I have a choice:
Live as a happy backwoods king for aye;
Or give the world an everlasting murmur of my name,
And die.
    Be up tomorrow sharp
To see me sacrifice to Lord Poseidon and set sail.
    Oh, yes, his gifts:
"The greatest benefaction ever known."
    If he put Heaven in my hand I would not want it.

His offers magnify himself.

    Likewise his child.

I do not want to trash the girl.

She is like me. Bad luck to have poor friends.

Bad luck to have his kingship as your sire.

    My father will select my wife.

Each spring a dozen local kings drive up

And lead their daughters naked round our yard.

Some decent local girl. My father's worth

Is all the wealth we will require.

    You Greeks will not take Troy.

You have disintegrated as a fighting force.

Troy is your cemetery. Blame your King.

The man who you say has done all he can.

The man who has admitted he was wrong.

But he has not done all he can.

And he has not admitted he was wrong.

Or not to me.

    I want him here, your King.

His arms straight down his sides, his shoulders back,

Announcing loud and clear that he was wrong to take my she.

Apologising for that wrong, to me, the son of Péleus.

Before my followers, with you, Pylos and Salamis,

Crete. Sparta. Tyrins, Argos, Calydon, the Islands, here,

Stood to attention on either side of him.

    That is *my* offer. Take it, or die.

    'Nestor may stay the night.

You, dear cousin Ajax, tell your King what I have said.

Preferably, in front of everyone.'

                        Who said,

As my Achilles lifted his guitar:

    'Lord, I was never so bethumped with words

Since first I called my father Dad.'

WAR MUSIC

An Account of Books 16–19

Patrocleia

Now hear this:
While they fought around the ship from Thessaly,
Patroclus came crying to the Greek.

   'Why tears, Patroclus?' Achilles said.
'Why hang about my ankles like a child
Pestering its mother, wanting to be picked up,
Expecting her to stop what she is at,
Getting its way through snivels?
   You have bad news from home?
Someone is dead, Patroclus? Your father? Mine?
But news like that is never confidential.
If such were true, you, me, and all the Myrmidons
Would cry together.
   It's the Greeks, Patroclus, isn't it?
You weep because some thousand Greeks lie dead beside their
      ships.
But did you weep when those same Greeks condoned my wrongs?
If I remember rightly you said nothing.'

   And Patroclus:
'Save your hate, Achilles. It will keep.
Our cause is sick enough without your grudging it my tears.
   You know Merionez is wounded?
Lord Thoal, too – his thigh: King Agamemnon, even. Yet
Still you ask: *Why tears?*"
   Is there to be no finish to your grudge?
Please do not shrug me off. Mind who it is that asks,
Not the smart Ithacan. Not Agamemnon. Me.
And God forbid I share the niceness of a man
Who when his friends go down sits tight

225

And finds his vindication in their pain.
   They are dying, Achilles. Dying.
Think, if you cannot think of them, of those
Who will come after them. What they will say:
   Achilles the Resentful – can you hear it?
Achilles, strong? . . . *The Strongest of the Strong* – and just as well
Seeing his sense of wrong became so heavy.
   Shameful that I can talk to you this way.'
   All still.
   'Let me go out and help the Greeks, Achilles.
Let me command your troops. Part of them, then?
And let me wear your bronze.'
   Still.
   'Man – it will be enough!
Me, dressed as you, pointing the Myrmidons . . .
The sight alone will make Troy pause, and say:
"It's him." A second look will check them, turn them,
Give the Greeks a rest (although war has no rest) and turned.
Nothing will stop us till they squat behind their Wall.'

   And so he begged for death.

   'Why not add Agamemnon to your argument?' Achilles said.
'King vain, King fretful, greedy Agamemnon,
He did not come to see me here,
To ask my aid.
   Go on . . . *"He was a sick man at the time, Achilles.*
He did it to avoid unpleasantness, Achilles.
Achilles, he was not too well advised."'
   Staring each other down until he said:
   'O love,
I am so glutted with resentment that I ache.
   Tell me, have I got it wrong?
Didn't he take my ribbon she? –
Didn't his widow lords agree

That she was mine by right of rape and conquest? Yet
When it comes to it, they side with him:
The King who robs the man on whom his crown depends.
    Yet done is done. I cannot grudge for ever.
Take what you want: men, armour, cars, the lot.'
    Easy to see his loss was on the run,
Him standing, saying:
    'Muster our Myrmidons and thrust them, hard,
Just here' – marking the sand – 'between the enemy
And the Fleet.
    Aie! . . . they are impudent, these Trojans . . .
They stroke our ships,
Fondle their slim black necks, and split them, yes –
Agamemnon's itchy digits make me absent,
My absence makes them brave, and so, Patroclus,
Dear Agamemnon's grab-all/lose-all flows.
    All right: if not Achilles, then his vicar.
Forget the spear. Take this' – one half its length – 'instead.
You say Merionez is out? Bad. Bad. And Ajax, too? Far worse.
No wonder all I hear is
    Hector, Hector, Hector, everywhere Hector,
As if he were a god split into 60.
    Hurry, Patroclus, or they will burn us out . . .
But listen first. Hard listening? Good.
    Hear what I want:
My rights, and my apologies. No less.
And that is all. I want the ships saved. Yes.
Concurrently, the Panacheans, here,
At our tent: Crete, Pylos, Sparta, Calydon, Mycenae,
My cousin Ajax, if he has the time.
And if they cannot come on foot, on stretchers, crutches, frames,
With her, Briseis, mint, among them. Clear?
As for his gifts . . . well, if he deserves a favour,
We shall see.
    One other thing before you go:

227

Don't overreach yourself, Patroclus.
Without me you are something, but not much.
Let Hector be. He's mine – God willing.
In any case he'd make a meal of you,
And I don't want you killed.
But neither do I want to see you shine at my expense.
   So mark my word:
No matter how, how much, how often, or how easily you win,
Once you have forced the Trojans back, you stop.
   There is a certain brightness in the air.
It means the Lord Apollo is too close
For you to disobey me and be safe.
   You know Apollo loves the Trojans; and you know
That even God, our Father, hesitates
To check the Lord of Light.
   O friend,
I would be glad if all the Greeks lay dead
While you and I demolished Troy alone.'

Cut to the strip between the rampart and the ditch.

   The air near Ajax was so thick with arrows, that,
As they came, their shanks tickered against each other.
And under them the Trojans swarmed so thick
Ajax outspread his arms, turned his spear flat,
And simply *pushed*. Yet they came clamouring back until
So many Trojans had a go at him
The iron chaps of Ajax' helmet slapped his cheeks
To soft red pulp, and his head reached back and forth
Like a clapper inside a bell made out of sword blades.
   Maybe, even with no breath left,

Big Ajax might have stood it yet; yet
Big and all as he was, Prince Hector meant to burn that ship,
And God was pleased to let him.

   Pulling the Trojans back a yard or two
He baited Ajax with his throat; and Ajax took.
As the spear lifted, Hector skipped in range;
As Ajax readied, Hector bared his throat again;
And, as Ajax lunged, Prince Hector jived on his heel
And snicked the haft clean through its neck
Pruning the eighteen-incher – Aie! – it was good to watch
Big Ajax and his spear blundering about for, O,
Two seconds went before he noticed it had gone.
   But when he noticed it he knew
God stood by Hector's elbow, not by his;
That God was pleased with Hector, not with Ajax;
And, sensibly enough, he fled.

   The ship was burned.

October
The hungry province grows restive.
The Imperial army must visit the frontier.
Dawn.
The captains arrive behind standards;
A tiger's face carved on each lance-butt.
And equipment for a long campaign
Is issued to every soldier.
First light.
Men stand behind the level feathers of their breath.
A messenger runs from the pearl-fringed tent.
The captains form a ring. They read.
The eldest one points north. The others nod.

Likewise his heroes stood around Achilles, listening.
And the Myrmidons began to arm and tramp about the beach.
First sunlight off the sea like thousands of white birds.

Salt haze.

Imagine wolves: an hour ago the pack
Hustled a stag, then tore it into shreds.
Now they have gorged upon its haunch
They need a drink to wash their curry down.
So, sniffing out a pool, they loll their long,
Thin, sharp-pointed tongues in it; and as they lap
Piping shadows idle off their chops,
And infiltrate the water like rose smoke.

Likewise his Myrmidons,
Their five commanders, right,
Patroclus on his left,
And the onshore wind behind Achilles' voice:

'Excellent killers of men!
Today Patroclus leads; and by tonight,
You, behind him, will clear the Trojans from our ditch.
And who at twilight fails to bring
At least one Trojan head to deck the palings of our camp
Can sleep outside with Agamemnon's trash.'

The columns tightened.
The rim of each man's shield
Overlapped the face of his neighbour's shield
Like clinkered hulls – as shipwrights call them when they lay
Strake over strake, caulked against seas.
As they moved off, the columns tightened more;
And from above it seemed five wide black straps
Studded with bolts were being drawn across the sand.

Before Achilles sailed to Troy
Patroclus packed and put aboard his ship
A painted oak box filled with winter clothes;
Rugs for his feet, a fleece-lined windcheater –
You know the sort of thing. And in this box
He kept an eye-bowl made from ivory and horn
Which he, and only he, used for communion.
  When he had spoken to his troops he took it out,
Rubbed sulphur crystals on its inner face,
Then washed and dried his hands, before,
Spring water rinsed, brimming with altar-wine,
He held it at arm's length, and prayed:

> 'Our Father, Who rules in Heaven,
> Because Your will is done where will may be
> Grant me this prayer
> As You have granted other prayers of mine:
> Give my Patroclus Your victory;
> Let him show Hector he can win
> Without me at his side;
> And grant, above all else, O Lord,
> That when the Trojans are defeated, he
> Returns to me unharmed.'

God heard his prayer and granted half of it.
Patroclus would rout the Trojans; yes:
But not a word was said about his safe return.
No, my Achilles, God promised nothing of the kind,
As carefully you dried your cup,
As carefully replaced it in its box,
Then stood outside your gate and watched
Your men and your Patroclus go by.

Hornets occasionally nest near roads.
In the late spring they breed, feeding their grubs
And feeding off the tacky sweat those grubs exude.
Ignorant children sometimes poke
Sticks into such a nest, and stir. The hornets swarm.
Often a swollen child dies that night.
Sometimes they menace passers-by instead.

No such mistake today.

Swarming up and off the beach
Patroclus swung the Myrmidons right at the ships.
Keeping it on their right they streamed
Along the camp's main track; one side, the battered palisade;
On the other, ships.
Things were so close you could not see your front;
And from the footplate of his wheels, Patroclus cried:
'For Achilles!'
As the enemies closed.

The Trojans lay across the ship
Most of them busy seeing that it burned.
Others slid underneath and were so occupied
Knocking away the chocks that kept it upright
They did not see Patroclus stoop.
But those above did.
In less time than it takes to dip and light a match
Achilles' helmet loomed above their cheeks
With Myrmidons splayed out on either side
Like iron wings.
Dropping the pitch
They reached for javelins, keelspikes, boat-hooks, Kai!
Anything to keep Achilles off –
Have he and Agamemnon patched things up?

Patroclus aimed his spear where they were thickest.
That is to say,
Around Sarpedon's chariot commander, Akafact.
  But as Patroclus threw
The ship's mast flamed from stem to peak and fell
Lengthwise across the incident.
  Its fat waist clubbed the tiller deck
And the long pine hull flopped sideways.
  Those underneath got crunched,
And howling Greeks ran up
To pike the others as they slithered off.
  This fate was not for Akafact.
Because the mast's peak hit the sand no more than six
Feet from Patroclus' car, the horses shied,
Spoiling his cast. Nothing was lost.
  As Akafact fell back, back arched,
God blew the javelin straight; and thus
Mid-air, the cold bronze apex sank
Between his teeth and tongue, parted his brain,
Pressed on, and stapled him against the upturned hull.
His dead jaw gaped. His soul
Crawled off his tongue and vanished into sunlight.

  Often at daybreak a salty moon
  Hangs over Ida; and the wind that comes
  Over the curve of the world from Asia
  Knocks a tile off Priam's roof.
  About this time each day for nine long years
  His men marched down the Skean road,
  Their spears like nettles stirred by wind.
  And round about this time each day
  The Greek commanders shade their eyes
  And squinny through the morning sun.
  And since no battle has returned
  All of its soldiers, the Trojans wave,

Look back towards the Wall, and think
Of those who may require new men next day.

Within, then through, then in around outside the drooping gates
The battle swayed.
   Half-naked men hacked slowly at each other
As the Greeks eased back the Trojans.
   They stood close;
Closer; thigh in thigh; mask twisted over iron mask
Like kissing.
   One moment 50 chariots break out; head for the ditch;
Three cross; the rest wheel back; vanish in ochre dust.
For an instant the Greeks falter. One is killed. And then
The Trojans are eased back a little more;
The ship is saved, the fire smothered, and who cares
That Hector opens a new way,
Now moving, pausing now, now moving on again,
And his spear's tip flickers in the smoky light
Like the head of a crested adder over fern?
Always the Trojans shift towards the ditch.
   Of several incidents, consider two:
Panotis' chariot yawed and tipped him
Back off the plate by Little Ajax' feet.
Neither had room to strike; and so the Greek
Knocked his head back with a forearm smash
And in the space his swaying made, close lopped.
Blood dulled both sides of the leafy blade.
Fate caught Panotis' body; death his head.
   Nearer the ditch Arcadeum met Lycon:
Catching each other's eye both cast, both missed,
Both ran together, and both struck; but
Only Lycon missed both times.
   His neck was cut clean through

Except for a skein of flesh off which
His head hung down like a melon.

You will have heard about the restless mice
Called lemmings; how, at no set time, and why,
No one is sure, they form a grey cascade that pours
Out of the mountains, down, across the flat,
Until they rush into the sea and drown.

Likewise the Trojans as they crossed the ditch.

From the far bank Hector tried to help them.
Impossible . . .
    He did not guess
So many cars, so many infantry, had crossed;
Engaged, there never seemed enough; but now
They crammed the edge,
The big-eyed horses rearing at the drop,
Their mouths wrenched sideways,
Neck yokes dragged back like saddles.
    And though the drivers looped their reins,
Pegged themselves in, and hauled,
The teetering jam eased forward.
    Only the soft edge held them;
And as the wheels notched into it, the dirt came up
Over the bolts that pinned the axles to the centre-poles,
Horses on one side of the rim,
Cars and men the other.
    Stuck.
While other men, infantry,
Meant to be rearguard, climbed into, pulled friends into,
Shouted, struck at who tried to check them, jammed
Spear-poles through spokes –
    Aie . . .
And Patroclus let them, let them,

235

Let them balance, let them, then cried:
    'For Achilles!'
And drove in.
    So the Trojans nearest to Patroclus squirmed
Away from him towards the ditch; and those
Near falling into it clawed back
Towards Patroclus; and those cram-packed between
Just clawed and squirmed until
The soft edge gave, and Ilium's chariotry
Toppled into the ditch like swill.

On certain winter days the land seems grey,
And the no-headroom left between it and the grey
Masses of downthrust cloud fills with wet haze.
Lines of cold rain weld mile on sightless mile
Of waste to air. Floods occupy the state. And still
The rains continue, grey on grey.
God's punishment, say some, on those who bear
False witness, and some say, on those
Judges divorced from justice by contempt
Of those they judge: plus the accomplices of both
Perched on their fencing through the vacant day,
Until the water takes them all in all
In one enormous wave into the sea.

The Trojan horses made like this.
As they went up the far side of the ditch
They dragged behind them dead or half-dead charioteers
Looped in their reins.
Better like this, perhaps, than left to Greeks.

    Patroclus split the rump.
Some (only a few) followed their horses up

Onto the plain and ran for Troy. The rest
Scurried along the ditch and hid themselves
Among Scamander's fens.

   Nothing was left of Hector's victory except
Loose smoke-swaths like blue hair above the dunes,
And Panachea's ditch stained crimson where
Some outraged god five miles tall had stamped on glass.

   A movement in the air. Gulls lift;
Then sideslip; land again. No more.
Mindless of everything Achilles said
Patroclus went for Troy.

   See if you can imagine how it looked:

   An opened fan, held flat; its pin
(Which marks the ditch) towards yourself; its curve
(Which spans the plain) remote.
The left guard points at Troy; the right
Covers the dunes that front the Aegean coast.
Like crabs disturbed by flame the Trojans run
This way and that across its radiants.
Patroclus thrusts his fighters at the mid
Point of the pleated leaf; a painted sun.

   And it was here that Thestor, Enop's boy,
Met that circumstance in nature
Gods call Fate, and on this day, men called Patroclus.
   Thestor was not a Trojan.
But when King Priam's satraps came from Troy
And asked Sarpedon, Lycia's Prince, for aid,
And he said, 'Yes' – Thestor, the light in Enop's eye,

Applied to leave his management and fight,
And as he reined away, he called:
    'Do not forsake me, O my seven meadows,
Until I conquer Greece!'
Though all he conquered was six foot of sand.

    Fate's sister, Fortune, favours those
Who keep their nerve.
Thestor was not like this.
He lost his head, first; then his life.
    His chariot bucked too slow over the rutted corpses,
And as Patroclus drew abreast of him
The terrified boy let the horses baulk,
Leaving the reins to flow beside the wheels,
And cowered inside its varnished bodywork,
Weeping.
    They passed so close that hub skinned hub.
Ahead, Patroclus braked a shade, and then,
And gracefully as men in oilskins cast
Fake insects over trout, he speared the boy,
And with his hip his pivot, prised Thestor up and out
As easily as later men
Disengage a sardine from a tin.

    Nine more Lycians died on the long run for Troy,
And they were no great trouble.
    If a spear missed, Patroclus watched
Their white heels flutter up the plain through dust,
Picked a fresh haft, waited, then pinned his next.
    The day seemed done; dust could be left to dust;
Flies had laid eggs in many of the dead;
Until Sarpedon wedged his car across the rout,
Pushed up his mask, and said:
    'Well run, my Lycians, but from what?'
Selecting two light javelins. 'Who will wait

To see a hero spit
Once and for all this big, anonymous Greek?'
And vaulted off his chariot plate,
'That makes you sweat?' then flexed himself,
Running his thumb across his points, and scuffed
Dirt towards Patroclus, who climbed down
More slowly; pleased beneath his iron.

It was noon.

God and His wife (who is His sister, too)
Watched them prepare. He, with regret; she,
With satisfaction heard Him out:
  'Surely Fate has marked enough good men without Sarpedon?
Shall I return him to his waving plains
Or let . . .'
  And she:
  'Others beside Yourself have children due today.
If one god saves his bud – why not the rest?
  My dear, I know You love Sarpedon, and I know
His death goes hard. Why not do this:
Let him fight bravely for a while; then, when
Patroclus severs him from care and misery,
Sleep and Death shall carry him to Lycia by Taurus,
Remembered by wise men throughout the world,
And buried royally.'

Noon. Striped mosquitoes. Nothing stirs.

Under the white sun, back and forth
Across a disk of yellow earth, midway
Between the sea and the closed stone capital,
The heroes fought like Pharaoh's bare-necked hens
Wrangling over carrion in the air.

239

They sight each other, stand on their tails,
Lock claws, lie back inside their wings, and hang
High in between the white-faced pyramids
Each savaging the other's craw.

Likewise the human champions before
Patroclus' spear nosed past Sarpedon's fearless heart
And the ground sense in his body leached away.
   Kneeling at first, then laid full length,
Teeth clenched and saying: 'Gray, be quick
Or they will strip me while I live.
   And if my captured weapons prove their jubilee,
Shame on you, duke, until your dying day.
   So get our best.
Anaxapart, and Hagnet, Hector, too – do not miss him –
And cover me with moving blades till sunset.
Then . . .' he was going,
'For my sake, fighter . . .' going,
'Kill!'
   And he was gone.
Sunlight reflecting in his dry brown eyes.
   Patroclus in his chariot again,
Wiping his neck, his smiling beard,
About to signal the advance.

   'Listen, Master!'
Gray prayed to Lord Apollo,
   'Wherever you may be,
   And you are everywhere,
   And everywhere you hear
   Men in their trouble,
   Trouble has come to me.
   Our best is dead and I
   Am wounded, Lord!
   O Lord Apollo hear my prayer!

You know me, and you know
That I shall fight until I die.
But I can barely lift my arm!
Lord, put my pain to sleep
And grant me strength enough to sweep
My pike across Sarpedon's corpse
Until the sun obeys your call to set.'

And Apollo, Mousegod, Lord of the Morning, he
Whose face is brighter than a thousand suns,
Mollified his wound with sacred thought,
And let delight in fighting warm his loins.
And he did more: as Gray corralled their best,
Apollo called: 'Sun, stand thou still over Ilium,
And guard Sarpedon's body till their blades
Move over it as grasses over stone.'

    Air into azure steel;
The daylight stiffens to translucent horn;
    And through it
Falling
    One sun's cord
That opened out into a radiant cone around Sarpedon's corpse;
And him inside that light, as if
A god asleep upon his outstretched hand.

Dust like red mist.
Pain like chalk on slate. Heat like Arctic.
The light withdrawn from Sarpedon's body.
The enemies swirling over it.
Bronze flak.
    Man against man; banner behind raised banner;
The torn gold overwhelming the faded blue;

241

Blue overcoming gold; both up again; both frayed
By arrows that drift like bees, thicker than autumn rain.
   The left horse falls. The right prances through blades,
Tearing its belly like a silk balloon.
And the shields inch forward under bowshots.
And under the shields the half-lost fighters think:
We fight when the sun rises; when it sets we count the dead.
What has the beauty of Helen to do with us? Half lost,
With the ochre mist swirling around their knees,
They shuffle forward, lost, until the shields clash:
   – AOI!
   Lines of black ovals eight feet high, clash:
   – AOI!
And in the half-light who will be first to hesitate,
Or, wavering, draw back, and Yes! . . . the slow
Wavering begins, and Yes! . . . they bend away from us,
As spear points flicker between black hides
Bronze glows vaguely, and bones show like pink drumsticks.
   And over it all,
As flies shift up and down a haemorrhage alive with ants,
The captains in their iron masks drift past each other,
Calling, calling, gathering light on their breastplates;
So stained they think that they are friends
And do not turn, do not salute, or else salute their enemies.
   But we who are under the shields know
Our enemy marches at the head of the column;
And yet we march!
The voice we obey is the voice of the enemy;
Yet we obey!
And he who is forever talking about enemies
Is himself the enemy!

   If Hector waved,
His wounded and his sick got up to fight;
And if Patroclus called, the Myrmidons

Struck, and called back; with them, as with Patroclus,
To die in battle was like going home.

Try to recall the pause, thock, pause,
Made by axe blades as they pace
Each other through a valuable wood.
Though the work takes place on the far
Side of a valley, and the axe strokes are
Muted by depths of warm, still standing, air,
They throb, throb, closely in your ear;
And now and then you catch a phrase
Exchanged between the men who work
More than a mile away, with perfect clarity.

Likewise the sound of spear on spear,
Shield against shield, shield against spear
Around Sarpedon's body.

It is true that men are clever,
But the least of gods is cleverer than their best.
    And it was here, before God's hands
(Moons poised on either side of their earth's agate)
You overreached yourself, Patroclus.
    Yes, my darling,
Not only God was out that day but Lord Apollo.
'You know Apollo loves the Trojans: so,
Once you have forced them back, you stop.'
    Remember it, Patroclus? Or was it years ago
Achilles cautioned you outside his tent?
    Remembering or not you stripped Sarpedon's gear
And went for Troy alone.

And God turned to Apollo, saying:
'Mousegod, take My Sarpedon out of range
And clarify his wounds with mountain water.
Moisten his body with tinctures of white myrrh
And violet iodine; and when these chrisms dry
Fold him in miniver that never wears
And lints that never fade,
And call My two blind footmen, Sleep and Death,
To carry him to Lycia by Taurus,
Where, playing stone chimes and tambourines,
The Lycians will consecrate his death,
Before whose memory the stones shall fade.'
   And Apollo took Sarpedon out of range
And clarified his wounds with mountain water;
Moistened his body with tinctures of white myrrh
And violet iodine; and when these chrisms dried
He folded him in miniver and lints
That never wear, that never fade,
And called God's two blind footmen, Sleep and Death,
Who carried him
Before whose memory the stones shall fade
To Lycia by Taurus.

Three times Patroclus reached Troy's Wall.
Three times he leapt towards its parapet.
Three times, and every time he tried it on
The smiling Mousegod flicked him back.
But when he came a fourth, last time,
The smile was gone.
   Instead, from parapet to plain to beach-head, on,
Across the rucked, sunstruck Aegean, the Mousegod's voice,
Loud as ten thousand crying together,
Cried:

'Greek,
Get back where you belong!'

So loud
Even the Yellow Judges giving law
Half-way across the world's circumference paused.

'Get back where you belong!
Troy will fall in God's good time,
But not to you!'

Patroclus fought like dreaming:
His head thrown back, his mouth – wide as a shrieking mask –
Sucked at the air to nourish his infuriated mind
And seemed to draw the Trojans onto him,
To lock them round his waist, red water, washed against his chest,
To lay their tired necks against his sword like birds.
– Is it a god? Divine? Needing no tenderness? –
Yet instantly they touch, he butts them, cuts them back:
– Kill them!
My sweet Patroclus,
– Kill them!
As many as you can,
    For
Coming behind you through the dust you felt
    – What was it? – felt Creation part, and then

APO

Who had been patient with you

Struck.

His hand came from the east,
And in his wrist lay all eternity;
And every atom of his mythic weight
Was poised between his fist and bent left leg.
    Your eyes lurched out. Achilles' bonnet rang
Far and away beneath the cannon-bones of Trojan horses,
And you were footless . . . staggering . . . amazed . . .
Whirled to the outskirts of the battlefield,
Between its clumps of dying, dying yourself,
Dazed by the brilliance in your eyes,
The noise – like weirs heard far away –
Dabbling your astounded fingers
In the vomit on your chest.
    And many wounded Trojans lay and stared at you;
Propped themselves up and stared at you;
Feeling themselves as blest as you felt cursed.
    All of them lay and stared;
And one, a hero boy called Thackta, cast.
His javelin went through your calves,
Stitching your knees together, and you fell,
Not noticing the pain, and tried to crawl away.

    No hope of that.

    Hector,
Standing above you,
Putting his spear through . . . ach, and saying:
    'Why tears, Patroclus?
Did you hope to melt Troy down
And make our women fetch the ingots home?
    I can imagine it!

You and your marvellous Achilles;
Him with an upright finger, saying:
    "Don't show your face to me again, Patroclus,
Unless it's red with Hector's blood."'
    And Patroclus,
Shaking the voice out of his body, says:
    'Big mouth.
Remember it took three of you to kill me.
A god, a boy, and, last and least, a prince.
    I can hear Death pronounce my name, and yet
Somehow it sounds like *Hector*.
    And as I close my eyes I see Achilles' face
With Death's voice coming out of it.'

    Saying these things Patroclus died.
And as his soul went through the sand
Hector withdrew his spear and said:
    'Perhaps.'

GBH

Before it disappears beneath the sea
The plain due west of Troy accumulates
Into a range of whalebacked, hairy dunes,
Two days' ride long, parallel to the coast,
And, at their greatest, half a bowshot thick.
White, empty beaches, supervised by Greece,
Stretch from the tidemark to their sandy cliffs;
But on the landward side, and long before
Their yellows fade through buff into the slope
And counterslope that stand before/beneath Troy's Wall,
Sickle-shaped bays of deep, loose sand, embraced
By corniced horns, appear; and close beside
– Much like the foothill of a parent range –
The knoll called Leto's Chair
Trespasses on the buff and masks the mouth
Of one such bay, in which
Patroclus lies and Thackta dreams:

    'I got his love. If I could get his head . . .'

Picture a yacht
Canting at speed
Over ripple-ribbed sand.
    Change its mast to a man,
    Change its boom to a bow,
    Change its sail to a shield:
Notice Merionez
Breasting the whalebacks to picket the corpse of Patroclus.

Thackta, get lost: he has not seen you – yet.
A child beheading parsley grass
Is all you'll be to him, who knows –
If he can get it out – Patroclus' corpse
Will break Achilles' strike, and vaults
The tufted hussock between you and him,
Then lets his long, grey, eighteen-inch-head spear
Sweep, sweep, Patroclus' vacant face: guarding him gone
Raptly as speechless breathers guard their young –
So run!
   But he does not. Prince Hector is his god.
Instead:
   'Cretan, get off my meat.
I got him first' (a lie) 'his flesh is mine.'
Smooth as a dish that listens to the void
Merionez' face swings up.
   Dear God, he thinks,
Who is this lily-wristed titch?
Picking a blob of dried froth from his lips,
Locking his mud-green eyes on Thackta's blue,
And saying: 'Boy,
I can hear your heart.
Who hoped to hold your children on her knee?'

   Whenever Thackta fought he wore
Slung from an oiled tendon round his neck
A cleverly articulated fish;
Each jacinth scale a moving part; each eye, a pearl.
His luck; his Christopher; a gift.
   'My name is Thackta, Crete,' he said,
And fingered it.
   'Thackta, the son of Raphno, lord of Tus?'
   'Indeed.'
   'And brother of lord Midon?'
   'Yes.'

254

'Here is the news. I killed him earlier today.
Not that his death was worth an ounce of fluff.'
    Answer him, Thackta; keep him at his chat;
We can see Hector; Hector reads your fix,
And will return before his king-sized wart
Upon the body of your world can cast,
So do not cast . . . And yet he does,
And notes – arm up, toe down – the spear approach
Merionez' needling mouth, who wills it near,
Observes it streaking through the sunburnt air,
Waits till its haft is half that haft's length off,
And shears it skyward with his own.
Then grabbed the tendon around Thackta's neck,
And slammed his downwards moving cry against his knee,
And poached his eyes, and slammed and slammed
That baby face loose as a bag of nuts, and when
Young Thackta's whimpering gained that fine, high scream
Dear to a mind inspired by violence, the Cretan duke
Posted his blade between the runny lips,
Increased the number of the dead by one,
Eased his malignant vigour with a sigh,
And scratched. Then snapped the thong
And wiggled Thackta's jacinth fish
Between the sun and his victorious eye.

No sound. No movement in the bay.
Stripping his victim with professional speed,
Plate-straps between his teeth, Patroclus up,
And, hup! Knees bowed. One last look round.
Now up the whalebacks to the coast.

    Not your day, king Merionez, not your day:
Dust in the air? or smoke? a shout –

Source out of sight, but near, but out of sight
Behind the crest, trough, crest, trough, crest,
Now soon, now soon to see
– Put down that armour, isolated lord –
Hector with Gray, Chylabborak, Anaxapart,
Outdistancing the wind that comes from Greece:
    'If I leave you, Patroclus, what?'
And Hector's blood-cry, Hector's plume
    'If I do not, what will become of me?'
Among the other, nodding plumes;
And all their banners rising one by one,
One after one, and then another one:
    'Prince Hector's one of them,'
Come between Leto's Chair, the corniced horn,
Fast as a viper over bathroom tiles,
Into the yellow bay.
    Bronze tyres. Reflecting breast-straps. You must set
Patroclus' body back upon the sand,
And as the arrows start to splash, back off,
Running towards the backslope, up, a cat,
Airborne a moment, one glance back: 'Dear God,
Their chariots will slice,' splash, 'the corpse,' splash, splash,
'In half,' and reach the crest,
And:
    'Ido!'
And:
    'Odysseus!'
You shout, and run, and run . . .
    And who would not?
    Then Hector's hand goes up.
Up go the horses. Zigzagged sand. Wheels lock.
    And you are off,
As he climbs down.

Eyelight like sun on tin.
   'My lord?'
Turning Patroclus over with his foot,
   'Yes, Gray?'
   'The Greek has gone for help.'
   'I know,'
His nostrils fluttering,
   'Give me your axe,'
His mouth like twine.
   'My axe?'
   'You – Manto.
Shell this lookalike and load the armour up.'
   Tall plumes go bob.
   'And you –'
(Sarpedon's armourer)
   'Anaxapart,'
(Who once had 50 stitches in his face)
   'Up with its shoulders. Yes, like that.'
(And you could strike a match upon the scar.)
   'Now stretch its neck across that rock,'
His arm held out behind; still looking down.
   'Lord Gray, I asked you for your axe.'
Zephyrs disturb their gilded crests. Mask meets mask.
Then Gray:
   'Before you use Patroclus' fat to grease
Your chariot hubs, Overlord Hector, ask yourself how
Troy can be held without Sarpedon's men.

   Dog in the forehead but at heart a deer,
Recall the luckless morning when you kicked
Your silk-and-silver counterpane aside
And found your coast alive with shrieking Greeks.

   After the shock of it, was not Sarpedon's name
The first to cross your lips? Whose help you begged?
Though all you sent was *"We would be obliged"*
And *"Thankyou, thankyou"* when he promised it –

Keeping his promise with half Lycia.
  And on the day we came,
Before Aeneas and yourself had stopped
Multiplying thanks by previous thanks,
Sarpedon and Anaxapart had struck.
  That day, and every long successive fighting day,
He was first out, last home; with laughter,
Golden wounds, good words; always the first,
First across Agamemnon's ditch today.
  But now that he is dead and has no fellow,
How do you keep your obligation, Hector?
  Begging my axe to violate the one Greek corpse
Sufficiently revered to change for his,
Wanting Achilles' gear to pod your beef,
Giving Merionez the time to fetch
More of our enemies up.
  I know . . . I know . . .
Day one, a friend; day two, a guest; day three, a chore.
  Sarpedon's death makes me the Lycian chief.
Why should we risk ourselves for Hector's Wall
Who leaves his ally naked in the dust?'

  Thin
Wavering heat. Big flakes of sand.
The tail-end of a banner wraps
A soldier's face.

  'You will not die saluting, Gray.'
And to the rest:
  'Get the bones home. When Greece comes back
I shall be good enough to watch.'

  Patroclus naked now.
Achilles' bronze beneath a chariot rug.

Manto beside the horses, eyes cast down,
Awaiting Hector's word.

'Lead on.'

Silent as men grown old while following sheep
They watch him and Chylabborak wheel away.

Sea-bird's eye view:
Soldiers around Patroclus: centaur ants
Hoisting a morsel,
  And,
On the whalebacks' tidal side,
Idomeneo, Ajax, Little A.,
Odysseus and Bombax head
A wedge of plate-faced Greeks.
  Close-up on Bombax; 45; fighting since 2;
Who wears his plate beneath his skin; one who has killed
More talking bipeds than Troy's Wall has bricks;
Whose hair is long, is oiled, is white, is sprung,
Plaited with silver wire, twice plaited – strong? –
Why, he could swing a city to and fro with it
And get no crick; whose eye can fix
A spider's web yoking a tent peg to its guy
Five miles downbeach – *and* count its spokes:
  'By night?'
  'No cheek.'
  See them come padding down the coastal lane,
Flow up the low-browed cliffs, across the whalebacks,
Two hundred plus. Then, at Odysseus' sign, drop flat,
And steer their plumage through the sabre grass,
Lining the shoulders of the bay to look
Down from the Chair at Gray beside the corpse.

'Ready?' Odysseus says.
Tall plumes go bob.

Moving at speed, but absolutely still,
The arrow in the air. Death in a man
As something first perceived by accident.
Massed hands, massed glare,
The piston-kneed, blade-flailing Greeks pour down
Like a gigantic fan with razored vanes,
Leaping the hummock-studded slope, up-down,
As if the ground between each clump were taut,
Were trampoline, up-down, so slow they fly,
So quick upon the sand.
   Gray, for an instant blinded by the sky
White backflash off their urns; but in the next,
Scanning them through its after-image, cool
As the atrium of a mossy shrine:
   'Close! Close!'
Too late. Before his voice is out
Their masks are on him like a waterfall.
   Who was it said
That one long day's more work will see it done?
Up to the waist in dead:
   'Dear Lord of Mice,' he prays,
   'Dear Lord,' his fighters dead,
   'By day,'
Their souls like babies rising from their lips,
   'A river in the sky,
   – Keep close! –
   By night, an Amazon.
Save us, and I will build a stone
   – Close! Closer still! –
   Temple that bears

260

– Now slope your shields! –
Shadows of deer at sunset and thy name.'
    Clenching his men about Patroclus' corpse.
Faced by a fly. All eyes. An egg with eyes.
    'We have it still!' (the corpse).
Arrows that thock, that enter eyes, that pass
Close as a layer of paint, that blind,
That splash about them like spring rain.

    Bombax takes heads
Like chopping twelve-inch logs for exercise;
Feathers of blood surround him like a nude
On decorative water.
    'Hector, where? –
Dog in the forehead but at heart a doe,'
As sunlight jumps from cheek to shiny cheek,
Eager to glorify their transience.
    'Not up the Chair, that way lies death,
Anaxapart,' who does not hear, his eyes
On Pyrop, 'the Corinthian Ham' (as Little Ajax christened him)
The richest and the fattest Greek
(A chariot factory plus numerous farms)
To sail to Ilium from Aulis, who
Looks behind him, half crouched down,
As timid and as fearful as a dog about to stool.
    'Run, Greek – run, run,'
Anaxapart insists. And (fool!) instead
Of burrowing among the shields, he does,
And running cries:
    'My mother is alone, and old, and sick,'
But what fear urged obesity held back.
    Six arrows in the Lycian's fist:
    'My' – one
    'Is' – two
    'And' – three

Then – four – five – six
In the air at once . . . Wi'eeee!
Even Odysseus paused to catch that trick.
    – And the arrows go so fast their shanks ignite!
    – And the hits make Pyrop flounce!
Six hammer blows upon his neck; and long before his voice,
So high, so piteous and profound, died out,
Anaxapart's keen zanies stripped his tin.
    Pleasure maybe
But not a sign of victory in this.

    The Lycians still have the corpse. Gray's sword
Bent as if seen through water, split tip hooked,
Both edges blunted on Greek flesh:
    'This is our end, my Lord,'
His feet go backwards, treading on the dead
That sigh and ooze like moss:
    'Heaven is silent.
    Earth does not confide.
    I turn around,
    The way to Troy is barred.'
Patroclus in their midst. Around him, shields.
Around the shields, the masks.
    'Close! Close!'

Achilles' armour was not made on earth.
Hephaestus Scientist yoked its dancing particles.
Deliberate inattention has
Only enhanced its light-collecting planes;
Into whose depth, safe, safe, amid the dunes,
Prince Hector looks, amazed, and strips his own;
Stands naked in the light, amazed, and lifts
Its bodice up, and kisses it; then holds it out,
And like a man long kept from water, lets

Its radiance pour down; and sees within
The clouds that pass, the gulls that stall,
His own hope-governed face, and near its rim,
Distorted as the brilliant surface bends
Its rivetless, near-minus weight away,
His patient horses, and his men.

   Then,
Through the azure vacancy in which
Our cooling onion floats; clouds long as lips,
God's lips above Mount Ida, saying:

   'Child,
Although your death is nearer than your nose
And nothing farther from your thoughts than death,
You look a picture. Take My word:
Dressed in the metal that the gods once gave
To lord Peleus, and that he, no longer worth a carrot,
Gave to that splendid semideity, his son,
I grant you one illustrious further day.
But in return, Prince of the Gate,
Your own return to Troy, and to Andromache,
Is forfeit.
   Never again shall Troy
Tally the Panacheans that you slew. And nevermore
When she has sponged you clean of enemy blood,
Will your Andromache towel you dry.
   Farewell, brave heart, accept My quantum boost,
Until Oblivion's resistless whisper bids
Its pulse – a drum between two torches in the night –
To follow your creation on its way.'

   Hector is in the armour. Boran lifts
A coiling oxhorn to his lips. And though

Its summons bumps the tower where Priam sits
Beside a lip that slides
Out of a stone lion's mouth into a pool,
The king is old and deaf, and does not move.

One thousand Trojan soldiers form a ring.
They link their arms; they breathe in unison;
Lay back their faces till each throat stands wide,
And wait. And wait. Then on the masterbeat,
Shatter the empyrean with a cry!
Then stamp! Then cry! Then stamp again! Then cry!
Cry overfollowing cry, concordant stamp
On stamp, until the far, translucent blue
Augments their promising to die, and strides
Forward to sunset on their: 'God for Troy!'
   Hector is in the middle of that ring;
Crouched on his toes; his knees braced wide; palms up;
White dactyls tigered; arms outspread.
And now his certain, triple-armoured mind
(By God, the holy metal, and his men)
Grows light, grows lucent, clarified for death.
And as their voices mix above their Prince,
He rocks from toe to toe; and as they stamp,
First one and then the other of his feet
Lifts from the sand; and as they lean and lead
Into a skip-step sunwise traipse around,
Though Hector keeps his body jack-knifed down,
Adding his voice to theirs he starts to turn
Counter their turn, to lift himself, to spin,
Becoming in their eyes a source, a sun,
A star, whose force is theirs, who leaps –
Unfolds his body in the air, and in the air
Unsheathes Achilles' sword and makes it sing . . .

See how they flow towards him, arms upraised,
Table their shields to keep his height aloft,
And cry again, and cry, and start to pour
Over the dunes, him spinning on that top,
Across the buff and onward to the bay,
Achilles' blade about his waist, so fast,
A cymbal struck by voices, shimmer struck,
Out of whose metal centre Hector's own,
Seething between his teeth, wails up the sky
On one insatiable note.
    And as his wail spread outward on the air,
And as the stolen armour ate the light,
Those fighting round Patroclus' body thought
Earth had upthrust a floe of luminous malt
That swamped their world and pitched the famous Greeks
Back to the crest and filled the bay with waves.
    And surfacing upon that molten sludge,
Gray in his arms, Prince Hector said,
As he wiped the crawling stains away:
    'Remember me?'
Aeneas going by so close
His slipstream pats their cheeks:
    'Remember me?'
And rings Patroclus with a horse-high
Set-too-close-for-the-point-of-a-spear's-tip
Wall of a hundred oxhide coffin-tops.

Impacted battle. Dust above a herd.
Trachea, source of tears, sliced clean.
Deckle-edged wounds: 'Poor Byfenapt, to know,' knocked clean
Out of his armour like a half-set jelly,
'Your eyes to be still open yet not see,' or see
A face split off,

Sent skimming lidlike through the crunch
Still smiling, but its pupils dots on dice.
    Bodies so intermixed
The tremor of their impact keeps the dead
Upright within the mass. Half dragged, half borne,
Killed five times over, Captol – rose with his oar,
Sang as his rapt ship ran its sunside strake
Through the lace of an oncoming wave – now splashed
With blood plus slaver from his chest to chin,
Borne back into the mass, itself borne back
And forth across the bay like cherry froth.
    Someone breaks out; another follows him;
Throws, hits, rides on; the first – transfixed –
Hauls on the carefully selected pole
Trembling within his groin, and drags
His bladder out with it;
Then doubles popeyed back into the jam.
    The Greeks swear by their dead. The Trojans by their home.
'Not one step back –' 'If I should die –' and does.
Water through water: who can tell whose red, whose roar
It is? Their banners overclouding one by one;
One after one; and then another one.

    Anaxapart has tied Patroclus' body to a shield:
Spreadeagled on its front
With Zeeteez and Opknocktophon as crucifers.
And much as their posterity will spurn
Vampires with garlic, ignorance with thought,
Those Trojans elevate his corpse and claim:
    'Gangway for Troy!'
While in the chariot length their idol gains,
With fingerbells and feathered necklacing,
Molo the Dancer from Cymatriax
Tugs at its penis as he squeaks:
    'Achilles' love!'

Trumpets behind the corpse. More Trojan masks.
Then tambourines and drums: 'Not one step back . . .'
But must! 'Troy!' 'Troy!' 'If I –' and does,
And all: 'Are these my arms,
So tired they go on, and on, alone?'

Seeking a quiet eddy in the flood.
Blood flowing from his nostrils. He who fights
Without the aid of anger says: 'Antilochos,
Run to the Fleet. Give Wondersulk our news.
His love is dead. His armour gone.
Prince Hector has the corpse. And as an afterthought,
That we are lost.'
    'Why me, Odysseus?'
    'That is the why. Now go –
And not so gloomy if you wish to please.'
    Antilochos removes his bronze, and then:
Fast as the strongest wing can fly
Between the twilight and the setting sun,
He goes.

Elsewhere late afternoon goes lazily enough.
And yawning as he leaves his tent
To sigh and settle back against a rope
(As some men settle into life
Quiet in quiet rooms, supplied
With all they need by mute, obedient hands)
Achilles: struggling to blimp
The premonitions of his heart:
    '*No matter how, how much, how often, or how easily you win –*
O my Patroclus, are you bitten off?'

Antilochos appearing through these words.
Standing before his lord of lords;
Of all alive, the man he most admired;
Whose word – that he should go through arrow-fire like rain –
He would obey unhesitatingly,
Weakening Odysseus' message to: 'Is gone.'

Down on your knees, Achilles. Further down.
Now forward on your hands and thrust your face into the filth,
Push filth into your open eyes, and howling, howling,
Sprawled howling, howling in the filth,
Ripping out locks of your long redcurrant-coloured hair,
Trowel up its dogshit with your mouth.
    Gods have plucked drawstrings from your head
And from the template of your upper lip
Modelled their bows. Not now. Not since
Grief has you by the neck, and sees you lift your arms to Heaven,
Then pistol-whips that envied face
As your prize shes – careless, disordered, knees giving way –
Rushed out to you, knelt down around you, close to you,
Slapping their bodies furiously, raising:
    'Eeeeeeeeeeeeeeeeeeeee . . .'
        'Eeeeeeeeeeeeeeeeeeeee . . .'
            'Eeeeeeeeeeeeeeeeeeeee . . .'
Antilochos among them, weeping among them,
Frightened that you, the first of men,
Might find an edge with which to give your throat a mouth,
Holding your wrists,
Your beating, broken heart throwing him right and left.
Scattering your shes.
    'Eeeeeeeeeeeeeeeeeeeee . . .'
        'Eeeeeeeeeeeeeeeeeeeee . . .'
            'Eeeeeeeeeeeeeeeeeeeee . . .'
You sank, throat back, thrown back; your voice
Thrown out across the sea to reach your source.

Salt-water woman
Eternal, his mother,
  Sheer-bodied Thetis who lives in the wave
  In the coral
  Fluorescent
Green over grey over olive for ever
  The light falling sideways from Heaven
She heard him
  Achilles
Her marvellous son.

  Surge in her body,
Head ferns grow wider,
  Grow paler,
Her message, his message
  Goes through the water:
  'Sisters,'
Nayruesay
  'Sisters,'
Eternal
  Salt-water women
Came when she called to them
Came through the waves to her, swam as she swam
Towards Greece, beyond Greece, now she passes the Islands,
Arm over arm swimming backways, peaked nipples,
Full 50 green-grey palely shimmering kith of Oceanayruce
Those who leave eddies, who startle, her sisters:
  Derna, Leucatay, lithe Famagusta,
Isso, Nifaria, black chevroned Cos,
Panopay, beaded, entwining Galethiel,
Thasos, Talitha, Hymno and Phylatte,
Sleek Manapharium, Jithis, Bardian, Proto and Doto,
Serpentine Xanthe, Nemix and Simi,
Came from the iodine, surfaced through azure

Stepped up the beach and enclosed
The sobbing Achilles.

'Why tears?' his mother said. 'I went to God.
And He has done all that you asked.
    It was your voice He heard, begging Him: "Lord,
Until they feel my lack, let the Greeks burn."'
    And heard him, in between his sobs, say:
    'I have killed Patroclus.
I have killed him. I have killed him. I have killed him.'
    'Eee . . . eee . . . eee . . . eee . . . eee . . .' a terrifying noise.
The like of which, the likes of you and me have never heard.
    'He was my best. Better than me. Braver than me.
More honourable than me. Worth twice my life.
He listened. He advised. Had time for everyone.
For men and women that I failed to see.
And I have killed him. I have killed him.'
    That terrifying noise. Those slaps.
    'I was not there to help him when he died.
I was not there to help him when he died.
Achilles was not there. He was not there
To help his next, his heart, his dear companion when Hector
        killed him.
    I know that God has said that I shall die
Soon after killing Hector – if I can.
And, mother, yes, be certain that I can.'

    'But cannot without armour, son,' she said
And vanished through the waves with all her school.

270

Sunfade. Sea breathing. Sea-lice trot
Over warm stones.
    Achilles and Antilochos:
How small they look beneath the disappearing sky!
Sap rises in them both. A breeze
Ruffles their hair; but only A. hears:
    'Greek . . .'
    'Yes?'
    'Greek . . .'
    'Who?'
    'Iris.'
    'Speak.'
    'Go to your ship.
Let Troy know you are back.
Until your strength is operational
Your voice must serve.
    You know what fighting is:
When things are at their worst
An extra shout can save the day.'

    He goes.

Consider planes at touchdown – how they poise;
Or palms beneath a numbered hurricane;
Or birds wheeled sideways over windswept heights;
Or burly salmon challenging a weir;
Right-angled, dreamy fliers, as they ride
The instep of a dying wave, or trace
Diagonals on snowslopes.

    Quick cuts like these may give
Some definition to the mind's wild eye
That follow-spots Achilles' sacred pair –

No death, no dung, no loyalty to man
In them – come Troyside down the dunes towards the Chair, the
    bay,
Achilles' charioteer, Alastor,
Pulling with all his might to make them stay,
That also Iris heard, that know their Care,
Achilles, will soon call.

Head-lock, body-slam,
Hector attacking.
    His anger, his armour, his:
'Now, now, or never, O Infinite, Endless Apollo,'
    But silent,
    'In my omnipotence I beg to cast
All thought of peace on earth for me away
Until I own that corpse.'
    Hard to say who is who: the fighters, the heroes,
Their guts look alike.

    Ajax alone between it and their thirst:
Pivoting on his toes, his arms looped up,
Safe in his hands his spear's moist butt, that whirrs
– Who falls into that airscrew, kiss goodbye –
And momentarily Prince Hector driven back,
And when, and if, and here it comes:

'On! On! On! On!' he cries. 'Die on that spear!'

    The Trojans try to snake beneath its point,
And Ajax down on one, and with the other foot
Thrusts himself round until the spear's bronze torque
Hisses a finger's width above Patroclus' face,
As Bombax shouts: 'To Ajax. Here,'
As Menelaos: 'Here . . .'

Gray sees Alastor entering the bay
Close under Leto's Chair, runs up the chair
Then springs towards its brink
And . . . off . . .
    Free fall –
    Free fall –
Swooping towards Alastor in his car,
As angels in commemorative stone
Still swoop on unknown soldiers as they die
For some at best but half-remembered cause.
    And as Alastor swerved, Gray's axe
Enhanced the natural crackage of his skull,
And he quit being, while his pair
Skid-slithered through the tumult, flailed that mass,
Then overran Patroclus' tattered corpse
Driving great Ajax off.

    Hector triumphant:
Dropping his spear, clenching his fists,
Raising his fists in the air, shaking his fists with delight:

    'Who brings it out will share the fame with me!'

    Anaxapart has got it by the chin.
Knees bent, spine bowed, feet braced into the clavicles,
Wrenching the head this way and that, thinks:
    'Screw the bastard off . . .'
Leaning across Anaxapart, Prince Hector shouts, 'On! On!'
Trying to slash at Bombax and the Greeks,
Who have Patroclus by the feet, and tug:
    'Ah . . .'
They tug.
    'Ah . . .'
The body stretched between them like a hide.

Look north.
Achilles on the forepeak of his ship.
   He lifts his face to 90; draws his breath;
And from the bottom of his heart emits
So long and loud and terrible a scream
The icy scabs at either end of earth
Winced in their sleep; and in the heads that fought
It seemed as if, and through his voice alone,
The whole world's woe could be abandoned to the sky.

   And in that instant all the fighting glassed.

   Thoal excepted.

   Quick as a priest who waits for passing birds
To form a letter in the air
He has Patroclus' body up and out.
   And as Prince Hector shouts:
'The Greeks have got their carrion intact!'
   The sun,
Head of a still-surviving kingdom, drew
The earth between them and himself,
   And so the plain grew dark.

Starred sky. Calm sky.
Only the water's luminosity
Marks the land's end.

   A light is moving down the beach.
It wavers. Comes towards the fleet.
The hulls like upturned glasses made of jet.

Is it a god?

No details

Yet.

Now we can hear a drum.

And now we see it:
Six warriors with flaming wands,
Eight veteran bearers, and one prince,
Patroclus, dead, crossed axes on his chest,
Upon a bier.

Gold on the wrists that bear the prince aloft.
Tears on the cheeks of those who lead with wands.
Multiple injuries adorn the corpse.
And we, the army, genuflect in line.

Four years ago Achilles robbed Kilikiax' citadel
And kept the temple cauldron for himself.
Talthibios read the inscriptions on its waist.
One said:
  I AM THE EARTH
The other:
  VOID.

And when from zigzagged ewers his shes
Had filled and built a fire beneath its feet,
Achilles laved the flesh and pinned the wounds
And dressed the yellow hair and spread
Ointments from Thetis' cave on every mark
Of what Patroclus was, and kissed its mouth,

And wet its face with tears, and kissed and kissed again,
And said: 'My love, I swear you will not burn
Till Hector's severed head is in my lap.'

Pax

R_{at.}
Pearl.
Onion.
Honey.
These colours came before the sun
Lifted above the ocean
Bringing light
Alike to mortals and Immortals.

   And through this falling brightness
Through the by now

Mosque
Eucalyptus
Utter blue,

Came

Thetis

   Gliding across the azimuth
With armour the colour of moonlight laid on her forearms,
Palms upturned,
Hovering above the Fleet,
Her face towards her son

   Achilles

   Gripping the body of Patroclus
Naked and dead against his own,
While Thetis spoke:

'My son . . .'
His fighters looking on;
Looking away from it; remembering their own:
    'Grieving will not amend what Heaven has done.
See what I brought . . .'
    And as she laid the moonlit armour on the sand
It chimed . . .
    And the sound that came from it
Followed the light that came from it
Like sighing
Saying:
    Made in Heaven.

    And those who had the neck to watch Achilles weep
Could not look now.
    Nobody looked. They were afraid.

    Except Achilles: looked,
Lifted a piece of it between his hands;
Turned it; tested the weight of it; and then
Spun the holy tungsten like a star between his knees,
Slitting his eyes against the flare, some said,
But others thought the hatred shuttered by his lids
Made him protect the metal.

    His eyes like furnace doors ajar.

    When he had got its weight
And let its industry assuage his grief:
    'I'll fight,'
He said. Simple as that. 'I'll fight.'

    And so Troy fell.

'But while I fight, what will become of this' –
Patroclus – 'mother?'
    And she:
'Son, while you fight,
Nothing shall taint him;
Sun will not touch him,
Nor the slimy things.'

    Promising this, she slid
Ichor into the seven openings of Patroclus' head,
Making the carrion radiant.
    And her Achilles went to make amends,
Walking alone beside the broken lace that hung
Over the sea's green fist.

    The sea that is always counting.

Ever since men began in time, time and
Time again they met in parliaments,
    Where, in due turn, letting the next man speak,
    With mouthfuls of soft air they tried to stop
    Themselves from ravening their talking throats;
    Hoping enunciated airs would fall
    With verisimilitude in different minds,
    And bring some concord to those minds; only soft air
Between the hatred human animals
Monotonously bear towards themselves.
No work was more regarded in our times,
And nothing failed so often. Knowing this,
The army came to hear Achilles say:
'Pax, Agamemnon.' And Agamemnon's: 'Pax.'

Now I must ask you to forget reality,
And be a momentary bird above those men
And watch their filings gather round
The rumour of a conference.
    From a low angle the army looks oval, whitish centred,
Split at one end, prised slightly open, and,
Opposite to the opening, Achilles,
(Whom they have come to hear) with hard-faced veterans
On either side, lance-butts struck down,
And here and there a flag. Even the chariot body-shop
Came to the common sand to hear their lords say pax.

    And as men will, they came, the limping kings;
Odysseus first, chatting to Menelaos, through the ring,
Sitting them down; and after them, a trifle slow
But coming all the same, Mycenae Agamemnon,
King of kings, his elbow gummed with blood.

    The ring is shut. Enormous calm.
King Agamemnon and Achilles face to face,
Distinct as polygon and square.

    Achilles:
    'King,
I have been a fool.
The bliss self-righteousness provokes
Addled my mind.'
    Odysseus nods.
    'Remembering my given she,
It would have been far better for us both
If Artemis had pinned her dead.
And doubtless as their mouths filled up with dust
The Greeks who died in my retirement
Wished the god had.
    Yet I'm a man. I like my own.

And if another man – my King, what's more –
Takes what is mine and lets the army know it,
What to do?
    Kings can admit so little.
Kings know: what damages their principality
Endangers all.
    If he is inconsiderate,
He is the King. If greedy, greedy King.
And if at noon the King says: *"It is night"* –
Behold, the stars!
    What if he damages the man
On whom his leadership depends?
He is still King. His war goes on. The man must give.
    But if the man in question cannot give
Because the god in him that makes the King his chief dependant
Is part and parcel of the god that cries *Revenge!* when he is
       wronged,
What happens then?
    Stamp on my foot, my heart is stunned.
I cannot help it. It is stunned. It rankles –
Here,' touching his chest.
    'I am not angry any more.
My heart is broken. Done is done, it says.
So let pride serve.
When all is said and done – I am Achilles.'

    And the army love their darling, and they cry:
    'Achil! Achil! Achil!'
Louder than any counting sea.
And sentries on the Wall sweat by their spears.

    King Agamemnon waits.

    And waits.

Then, rising, says:

'Heroes . . .
I do not think your zeal will be injured
If those who are the farthest off stand still,
And those in front stop muttering to themselves.'
    Bad start.
'Everyone can't hear everything, of course.'
    Gulls cry.
'However, even clear-voiced heralds,
Accustomed as they are to public speaking,
Can lose their audience if inattention makes them feel
Indifference to their message.'
    Gulls.

'In fact, the things I have to say are, in a sense,
Meant for Achilles' ears alone.
But if the army and his peers witness our settlement
My purpose will be better served.
    Like him, I am a man.
But I am also King. His King. Your King.
And as your King I have received
What most of you have not unwillingly agreed was mine:
The best part of the blame.'
    He has them now.
    'BUT I AM NOT TO BLAME!'
    And now.
    'Undoubtedly I took, unfairly, pulling rank,
The she that Achilles won.
    I tell you it was not my wish.
Between my judgement and my action Ahtay fell;
God's eldest girl, contentious Ahtay . . . Oh,
Soft are her footsteps but her performance keeps no day;
Nor does she walk upon the ground, but drifts
Into our human wishes like the sticky flecks of down

Tickling our lips in summertime,
And with her episode comes misery.
   Let me remind you how God walked
Into the courtyard of the sun and told His co-eternals:
   "Drink with me!
For unto men this day a child is born
Whose blood is royal with My eminence,
And who, all in good time, will be
A king called *Hercules*."
And looking at her fingers, Hera said:
   "We have been fooled before.
However; if You swear
That any child of Yours born on this day . . ."
God swore; and Ahtay sat between His eyes.
Soon as the oath had crossed His mythic lips
Hera went quick as that from Heaven to Greece,
And with her right hand masked the womb
Swaddling Hercules, and with her left
Parted the body of another girl whose child was His
But only eight months gone,
And held it up and jeered:
   "See what your oath has done!"
God made the early boy a king, and Hercules a serf,
And wept as men must weep.
   If you will fight again, Achilles,
I will return your she.'

   The sun is high.

   Achilles says: 'Let us fight now – *at once* – '

   'Wait' – slipping the word in like a bolt –
'Marvellous boy,' Odysseus says.
   'You can do what you like with us except make men fight
      hungry.
   Well . . . you could do that too, but . . .'

Turning away from him towards the ranks:
   'Wait!
The King will keep his promise now.
Young lords will fetch his penal gifts
For everyone to see and be amazed.
   Everyone knows that men who get
Angry without good reason will
Conciliate without gifts.
   Therefore Achilles gladly takes
Everything Agamemnon gives.
   And he who gives steps free of blame,
As he adopts the wrong.
   God bless them both.'

   Then, squatting by Achilles, says:
'Boy – you are the best of us. Your strength is fabulous.
But hear me out.
   What we have got to do is not embroidery.
For you, the battle may be gold.
The men will enter it like needles
Breaking or broken; either way
Emerging naked as they went.
   Think of the moment when they see
The usual loot is missing from this fight
Although the usual risks are not.
   They do not own the swords with which they fight,
Nor the ships that brought them here.
Orders are handed down to them in words
They barely understand.
They do not give a whit who owns queen Helen.
Ithaca's mine; Pythia yours; but what are they defending?
They love you? Yes. They do. They also loved Patroclus.
And he is dead, they say. Bury the dead, they say.
A hundred of us singing angels died for every knock
Patroclus took – so why the fuss? – that's war, they say,

Who came to eat in Troy and not to prove how much
Dear friends are missed.
Yes, they are fools.
But they are right. Fools often are.
   Bury the dead, my lord,
And I will help you pitch Troy in the sea.'

Cobalt in Heaven
And below it
   Polar blue.
The body of the air is lapis, and
   Where it falls
Behind the soft horizon
The light turns back to Heaven.

   A soldier pisses by his chariot.
Another
   Sweetens his axe blade on a soapy stone.
   And up between the dunes,
Their escorts lords Odysseus and Thoal,
Makon and Jica and Antilochos,
Come twelve white horses led by seven women
Briseis in their midst
Her breasts so lovely that they envy one another.
   And they pass by . . .
   And after them young lords escorting
Twenty ewers of bright silver each in a polished trivet
Their shining cheeks engraved by silversmiths
With files of long-nosed soldiers on the march.
   And they pass by . . .
   And after them a sledge
Piled with twelve lots of Asian gold
Carefully weighed, worth a small city.

And they pass by . . .
And last of all, guarding a sacrificial hog,
Talthibios passed by into the centre of the ring.

Yellow mists over Mount Ida.
The hog lowers its gilded tusks.
Is still.

By Agamemnon's feet Talthibios sprinkles barley,
Snips a tuft from the hog's nape,
Waits for a breeze to nudge it off his palm
Into the flames that burn between the army and its King.

Haze covers Ida.
Sand falls down sand.
Even the gods are listless.

And Agamemnon spreads his arms,
Raises his face towards the sun, and cries:

'GOD
Be my witness,
EARTH
My witness.
SUN, SKY, WATER, WIND
My witness.
While in my ownership
I did not tamper with the she
I took unjustly from Achilles.'

And as his great lords said

'Amen'

He dragged his knife across the hog's silk throat.

Mists over Ida.

The army like ten thousand yellow stones.

Achilles says:

'So be it.
Eat, and prepare to fight.'

And took Briseis to his ship.

Under the curve the keel makes
Where it sweeps upright to the painted beak
Achilles' heroes placed their gilded oars,
Set twelve carved thwarts across them,
Surfaced this stage with wolf- and beaver-fleece
Amid whose stirring nap Patroclus lay,
The damaged statue of a prince awaiting transportation.
   Near it Achilles sat, Odysseus beside,
And women brought them food.
   'Patroclus liked to eat,' Achilles said,
'And you cooked well, Patroclus, didn't you?
Particularly well that summer when
My cousin Ajax and king Nestor drove
Up from the Pel'ponnesus crying "wife"
And "theft" and "war" and "please" and –
What is this "eat" of yours, Odysseus?
If you were telling me: He's dead, your father; well,
I might eat a bit; troubled, it's true; but eat
Like any fool who came God knows how many mist
And danger mixed sea miles to repossess fair Helen.
   I know you, Ithaca: you think:
Achilles will fight better if he feeds.

Don't be so sure.

   I do not care about his gifts. I do not care, Odysseus,
Do not care.

   Patroclus was my life's sole love.
The only living thing that called
Love out of me.

   At night I used to dream of how, when he came home to
         Greece,
He'd tell them of my death – for I must die – and show my son,
This house, for instance, or that stone beside the stream,
My long green meadows stretching through the light,
So clear it seems to magnify . . .'

   And here Achilles, loved by God,
Was led by Sleep to sleep beside the stage,
And king Odysseus goes off as close to tears
As he will ever be.

Now I shall ask you to imagine how
Men under discipline of death prepare for war.
There is much more to it than armament,
And kicks from those who could not catch an hour's sleep
Waking the ones who dozed like rows of spoons;
Or those with everything to lose, the kings,
Asleep like pistols in red velvet.

   Moments like these absolve the needs dividing men.
Whatever caught and brought and kept them here
Is lost: and for a while they join a terrible equality,
Are virtuous, self-sacrificing, free:
And so insidious is this liberty
That those surviving it will bear
An even greater servitude to its root:
Believing they were whole, while they were brave;

That they were rich, because their loot was great;
That war was meaningful, because they lost their friends.
   They rise! – the Greeks with smiling iron mouths.
They are like Nature; like a mass of flame;
Great lengths of water struck by changing winds;
A forest of innumerable trees;
Boundless sand; snowfall across broad steppes at dusk.
   As a huge beast stands and turns around itself,
The well-fed, glittering army stands and turns.

   Nothing can happen till Achilles wakes.

He wakes.

   Those who have slept with sorrow in their hearts
   Know all too well how short but sweet
   The instant of their coming-to can be.
   The heart is strong, as if it never sorrowed;
   The mind's dear clarity intact; and then,
   The vast, unhappy stone from yesterday
   Rolls down these vital units to the bottom of oneself.

   Achilles saw his armour in that instant
And its ominous radiance flooded his heart.
   Bright pads with toggles crossed behind the knees,
Bodice of fitted tungsten, pliable straps;
His shield as round and rich as moons in spring;
His sword's haft parked between sheaves of grey obsidian,
From which a lucid blade stood out, leaf-shaped, adorned
With running spirals.
   And for his head, a welded cortex; yes,
Though it is noon, the helmet screams against the light;
Scratches the eye; so violent it can be seen
Across three thousand years.

Achilles stands; he stretches; turns on his heel;
Punches the sunlight, bends, then – jumps . . .
And lets the world turn fractionally beneath his feet.

Noon. In the foothills
Melons emerge from their green hidings.
Heat.

He walks towards the chariot.
Greece waits.

Over the wells in Troy mosquitoes hover.

Beside the chariot.
Leading the sacred horses; watching his this-day's driver,
    Automedon,
Cinch, shake out the reins, and lay them on the rail.
    Dapple and white the horses are; perfect they are;
Sneezing to clear their cool black muzzles.

He mounts.

The chariot's basket dips. The whip
Fires in between the horses' ears.
And as in dreams, or at Cape Kennedy, they rise,
Slowly it seems, their chests like royals, yet
Behind them in a double plume the sand curls up,
Is barely dented by their flying hooves,
And wheels that barely touch the world,
And the wind slams shut behind them.

'Fast as you are,' Achilles says,
'When twilight makes the armistice,
Take care you don't leave me behind
As you left my Patroclus.'

And as it ran the white horse turned its tall face back
And said:
    'Prince,
This time we will, this time we can, but this time cannot last.
And when we leave you, not for dead, but dead,
God will not call us negligent as you have done.'

    And Achilles, shaken, says:
'I know I will not make old bones.'

    And laid his scourge against their racing flanks.

    Someone has left a spear stuck in the sand.

BIG MEN FALLING A LONG WAY

Fragments from Books 10–24

It was the classicist Donald Carne-Ross, then working as a radio producer at the BBC, who got Christopher Logue hooked on Homer. Logue tells the story in his memoir, *Prince Charming* (1999). By his own account, the match was no *coup de foudre*. Looking back over forty years or more, he recalls how he needed a good deal of coaxing and tuition from Carne-Ross before he was able to produce his first Homeric text: a treatment of Achilles' fight with the river Scamander, based on the passage from Book 21 of the *Iliad*. In due course this was broadcast, printed in the magazine *Encounter*, and included in Logue's 1959 Hutchinson volume, *Songs*; but, because it fell outside the scope of his other Homeric titles, as they appeared over the following decades, it has not until now been seen in context, although it was given temporary housing in the *Selected Poems* of 1999. Yet it is a fully achieved piece of writing, boldly, even brazenly, establishing the rhetorical conventions and setting the artistic standards of what was to become not only Logue's principal creative preoccupation, the very heart of his writing life, but also one of the greatest – and, paradoxically, most original – poetic works in English of the last half-century.

Sadly, the poet never completed the project that in later years came to be referred to interchangeably as either *War Music* or *Logue's Homer* – the form of words that appeared on the front covers of, in turn, *War Music* (the 2001 edition), *All Day Permanent Red* (2003) and *Cold Calls* (2005), the last two volumes being subtitled *War Music continued*. It is clear, however, that, until illness stopped him, he had meant to finish the job. The numerous plans and schedules of the work as a whole that he was in the habit of drawing up as a writing aid demonstrate that he had a sense, albeit a fluctuating one, of what was needed to bring it to a conclusion; and in a letter of 12 August 2003 to his editor at

Faber & Faber, Paul Keegan, he offered this assessment of the final stages, totting up both what had been achieved and what was still to be done:

> It looks, roughly, like this:
>
> Patrocleia ⎫
> G.B.H.   ⎬ written
>   ⎭
> New armour / the Shield   unwritten
> Pax   written
>
> Achilles attacks
> Trojans driven back across the ditch to the Scamander
> Achilles fights the Scamander   mostly written
>   Achilles drives the Trojans back across the plain to Troy
>   Hector dies outside Troy   roughly written
>   Achilles defiles Hector's body, burns Patroclus'
>   corpse and sacrifices the 12 Trojan boys
>   Priam recovers Hector's corpse
>   Hector's corpse cremated after Hecuba, Andromache
>   and Helen have spoken.

It remains to be seen how this works out. It is rather a lot.

It would indeed have been rather a lot, but there is evidence that Logue had even more in mind. In the first of a series of ring binders labelled 'CONT. PLAN' – presumably 'Continuation Plan' – on their spines, there is a page which, under the heading 'Big Men – etc', lists, in addition to those passages itemised for Keegan's benefit, a run of earlier episodes that would have filled the large gap between *Cold Calls*, the most recently written volume, and 'Patrocleia', the first section of *War Music*. *Cold Calls* concludes with Nestor and Ajax's failed deputation to Achilles, and, in Homer, a lot happens, among both gods and humans, between that and the story of Patroclus' death.

The implication is that *Big Men Falling a Long Way* – Logue's working title for his projected final volume, and his own, witty definition of tragedy – would have done much more than simply to take Homer's narrative from *War Music* to the end. It would have subsumed the whole of *War Music* itself, adding both preceding and subsequent incidents, and inserting at least one detail of the story omitted from previous editions: the fashioning of Achilles' new shield and armour. In my own searches through Logue's working papers, I was sorry not to have found even a scrap of verse relating to this last item, especially as there is a tantalising note in prose, typed and pasted onto a page in 'CONT. PLAN 2', in which he suggests how his treatment will differ from Homer's: 'At the end of Book 18,' he writes, 'Homer describes the creation in Heaven of a new shield [. . .] The new shield's face is covered with designs that show the world as Homer knew it. This passage will be extended. The pictures on the shield will reflect our world.'

Homer's description of the shield is lavish and gorgeous enough; and yet Logue proposes to *extend* it. Poetic hubris? I do not think so. The magnitude of his ambition should not tempt anybody to suppose that he had bitten off more than he could chew. Large parts of *War Music* – sweeping surveys of the battlefield; individual feats of strength, speed and butchery; the overriding caprices of the gods – prove his capacity for the grand conception dashingly and convincingly executed. In those passages, too, where human vulnerability and pathos are the theme, he is equally up to the challenge; and in this respect I was particularly delighted to come across the long sequence, taken from Book 24, the last in the *Iliad*, where Priam goes humbly to beg Achilles for the return of Hector's body, and Achilles is so touched that, against all previous form, he accedes to the request. Logue's note to Keegan, above, suggests that he would have followed this with further material, as in Homer; but I wonder. It would be hard to see how any ending could be more effective, or affecting, than the one that, for want of the promised final scene, the present volume now has.

Putting together a 'definitive' edition of *War Music*, with its final instalment so far from completion, has presented the editor with a number of peculiar challenges. Most important to declare is the extent to which I have had, not just to find and rescue material for inclusion in *Big Men Falling* – that was the easy bit – but also to make certain arbitrary decisions as to the author's intentions, even in cases where it was likely that what he wanted was still unclear in his own mind. It must be understood that Logue was a habitual, even an obsessive, reviser of his work. Indeed, one of his finest and most original longer poems, 'New Numbers', may be said to have as its very *raison d'être* a fluid responsiveness to changing circumstances that would have prevented it from ever achieving a fixed state. Where his Homeric volumes were concerned, he amended and corrected long after publication. Thus, only a year after *Kings* came out, a 'Revised Edition' was considered necessary; *War Music*, published in 2001, had, in the three years before he dropped the Homer project once and for all, acquired, in the author's own copy, numerous insertions and marginalia that demonstrate his unresting dissatisfaction and so have been incorporated here; and even a passage as old and as often printed as the Achilles/Scamander episode was subject to continual tinkering.

More than that, Logue's method of composition means that notes, sketches, rough drafts, attempted fair copies – inevitably and immediately rendered doubtful by second and third thoughts – have proliferated promiscuously, all now vying for the editor's attention. There are dozens of MS pages which show the poet attacking this or that passage again and again, as if in the hope of knocking it into submission by just one final thrust. In addition to such abundance, the binders, folders and boxes that contain it contain much besides: synopses, also under constant revision; quotations from literary and ephemeral sources of different kinds; letters concerning work in progress, which may also include variant drafts or conflicting statements of intent; and more. All these, in the form of sheets from note-pads, pasted cuttings, photocopies, yellow stickies – even thriftily scissored yellow stickies! – share space with the supplementary material of which Logue was an avid collector: clippings from newspapers and magazines, for the most part, on a surprisingly wide range of topics, any detail of which might ultimately be fed into the on-going, juggernaut-like *magnum opus*. Running throughout, the poet's handwriting, tiny, but precise and beautiful, keeps its even pace, promising a safe, if necessarily hazardous and indirect, journey to some distantly promised landfall.

Access to these papers, which has been made possible to me through the kindness of the poet's widow, Rosemary Hill, has been a privilege and joy, as scholars of the future will no doubt confirm. The epic spirit of the enterprise speaks so eloquently through this material that one is moved to awe. But awe is not the most helpful emotion for an editor and I have, therefore, while piecing together the appendix to this volume, had to allow presumption to override it time and again. My ear is different from Christopher Logue's and, even if it is an ear capable of appreciating his 'war music', it is wary of trying to reproduce it. The reader can be reassured that the bulk of *Big Men Falling a Long Way* is pure Logue: that is, what the poet unambiguously intended at the moment of putting his words on paper, whether or not they would have stood unaltered until publication. My interventions, however, have been frequent – always based on textual evidence, but carrying an unavoidable element of presumption with them. My excuse? Simply, that even a partial and impaired glimpse of what should, in happier circumstances, have brought *Logue's Homer*, this great, Modernist act of poetic reimagining and reworking, to a conclusion, is better than no glimpse at all.

As for the books that have already been seen in print, the poet's own corrections and emendations have, of course, been followed. The reader will, however, notice anomalies and inconsistencies that have survived from printing to printing, and have not been touched by me. The poet's spelling of proper nouns – T'lesspiax, for instance, who elsewhere is either T'lespiax or Telespiax; or

Pandar, a.k.a. Panda – could be wayward, and his use of accents to indicate pronunciation was less reliable than he probably thought it was. There are oddities, too, in the punctuation that can't always be logically defended. While I occasionally felt a strong itch to put things right, or 'right', I decided that meddling in these cases would be an intervention too far. It is one thing, with fair warning, to patch together passages of still unfinished work with the purpose of giving the reader a hint, at the very least, of wonders that he or she might have enjoyed; quite another, to assume, in the poet's absence, the godlike right of a final buff and polish.

Christopher Reid

[*Iliad*, Book 10]

Behold the ordered army of the stars!
Their light across the north-Aegean sea:
The Greeks: their darkened beach-head: ships, tents, roads
Protected on their landwards side by
(Two spears high, a catwalk on its inner face)
A palisade: in front of that, a ditch,
And on the stretch of ground between it and the ditch
Lord Nestor and lord Ajax walking back
To Agamemnon of Mycenae, with bad news.

Lights.

Mycenae to his lords:

'Achilles has said *no*.
We have one chance: kill Hector. So
Sleep, and prepare to fight.'

'Ave!'

A thousand boat-cloaks disappear between the hulls.

Dawn.
Its lovely nothingness.
Dew shrinks on steel.

Topping the palisade
Some of the 20,000 masks that came to Troy from Greece nine
     years ago
See:

Hector
Aenéas, Gray, Chylábborak, Sárpedon
and

all Troy

They having crossed the ditch by night; now opposite their
     gates.

Then Hector's trumpets blare.

A path for him: we catch

His open look; his height
Between our shields; his smile; his easy stride;
The wide bridge of his shoulders, and – tense, tense –
That ancient, unaccountable demand,
     As through your window when a band plays by,
Making you want to follow him who says:

'All Souls:
Remember who you are.
Trojans. The Trojans. Those who fight for Troy.
For Troy! The city of God! The greatest city in the world!
Your fortress home.
     We face a horde of murderous criminals,
The universally detested Greeks.
They came to rape your wives, to loot your homes,
And then to burn our city, Holy Troy!
Give thanks to God, and to myself, your Prince,

Hector of Troy, King Priam's fighting son, they failed.
   And now we have them in our hands.
If they should try to launch their rotting ships
We fill their backs with spears.
To fight us means to leave their palisade.
To wait, means starve to death beside the sea.
   Trojans! – they are as good as dead.
But good as dead is not yet dead.
And that is what we want. We want them dead, dead, dead.
   It will be hard to kill them off
For they are desperate:
And there's no dying throw like desperation.
But we shall kill them. Every single one.
Chylábborak, my right, Aenéas on my left,
Your head, your leader and your heart, myself,
Hector of Troy, the Prince who Holds
The City, and the Plain and now the Coast.
   Rouse your brave hearts!
Be sure your battle-cries are heard in Heaven!
A farm that fills a valley, a wife from Priam's house,
For who is first across their palisade!
Praise Heaven – they advance!

   Delighted by this call to violence,
Wiping His eyes for those about to die,
God answered Hector's declamation with a thunderclap
That shook the Ilian coast.

   [']Living a mile below the snow-line
I am familiar with crevasses.
Up to 300 feet in depth, as much as 50 feet across,
Silent for years on end, one day
They groan, then groan again, and then again,
Not all that loudly, just loud enough
To make your hair prickle inside your hat.[']

This was the kind of sound that Troy
High on hope and Heavenly promises;
And Greece in its despair
Made as they drove themselves into each other's brutal arms.

Although notes and corrections in pencil cluster around it, the bulk of the text here, in CL's neatest and most decisive hand, is fairly clear, with moments of textual uncertainty multiplying only towards the end. Picking up from the return of the Greek deputation to Achilles, the failure of which concludes *Cold Calls*, these pages, or something close, were presumably intended to go at the beginning of *Big Men Falling a Long Way*.

Here and in following passages, the few spelling errors have been corrected silently. CL opens the penultimate stanza with inverted commas (changed here to a single inverted comma, in conformity with the rest of *War Music*), but fails to close with them. Square brackets indicate the editor's inability to decide what the author had in mind.

Some say: 'Every hedge has its gap.'
But as Greece came for us,
Trotting across the ground between the palisade and us,
There was no gap.
　　Shin deep in blood, we killed each other readily enough.
　　God clapped.
And swinging through the crush,
Their arms around each other's waists,
The Keres Sisters sang:
　　'We drink blood. We drink blood.
　　If we had our way we would
　　Drink ourselves to death on blood.'

　　Still on that ground,
Cherith – from Pindos, central Greece – a spear
Went into him just underneath the arm he raised to match his
　　　cheer. –
He had a donkey and his own front door. –
Those next to him fell back, but,
Still on that ground, Prince Hector shouting:
　　'Do I want revenge? I do!
Ten Greeks dead for every Trojan hurt.
Kill Greeks! Kill every Greek!' –
And if it was not Cherith gone, the Trojans moved
Forward an inch, then took another Ilian attack,
This upper-thrust, that pair of bugged-out eyes.
　　'Hero . . .'
This fast, firm swordarm, sss-sss, sss-sss, then
The point goes in, the air comes out.
　　'Ah . . .'
The blade turns in the wound, and then moves down.
　　'Fighters to *me* –' Odysseus. 'To *me*.'

      'My sword too short . . .'
      'Then add a step to it.'
      Still that same ground.
    Kazz – always camera-ready, killed
    Later that day while checking his appearance in a pool.
    Carts filled with logs to raise the palisade.

This passage – like the preceding one, also in ink – is headed 'Hector's first assault on the Greeks [*sic*] palisade'. Superimposed as it is, however, on an earlier pencil draft, it is in a markedly rougher and more unresolved state. Some of CL's marginalia have been absorbed by the editor into the printed text, while others, less easy to connect to the main body of the verse, have been ignored.

A note in pencil next to the lines about the 'Keres Sisters' reads: 'describe them? – who are they?' They are female spirits who represent the different terrible ways of dying.

[Unplaceable]

[1]

Take an industrial lift.
Pack it with men fighting each other,
Smashing each other back against its governors
So the packed cage shoots floors up, then down,
Then up again, then down, lights out, then stops,
But what does not stop are the blows,
Fists, feet, teeth, knees, the screams of triumph and of agony
As up they go, then stop, then down they go.
No place on earth without its god.

[2]

Sunshine; far out at sea,
Nothing except an aircraft-carrier in sight,
A plane just landed on its deck,
Its two-man crew loosening their helmet-straps.
Then, suddenly, but with no other change, there is a swell
And so the surface of the water lifts, the flight deck tilts,
The plane, and crew, slide overboard,
And on the unruffled sea the ship sails on.

These two isolated passages share a page with the heading 'Poss. Sims' – presumably 'possible similes', to be kept in reserve for some appropriate moment that never came. The first passage is almost entirely clean, with a single correction by CL himself; the second is the result of editorial negotiation between an initial draft in ink and CL's pencilled insertions.

A mile beyond Troy's shoreline is a deep,
And in that deep there is a cave,
And in that cave there is a throne,
And on that throne God's Brother, Lord Poseidon sits.
    But not this afternoon. This afternoon
His Majesty is out for a spin.
    Behold! –
His six-white-stallion-powered chariot
Streaming the aquamiles away – their spray
Falling around Him in a shower of stars!
    And the wind of His own speed ruffles His emerald hair,
And Californian rainbow-fish fly by
And Tritons, skinned like surf,
Trumpet His progress with their shells.

    Then every dweller of His fluent world
Surfaced to welcome Him; and by His car
Bare-chested Pan'o'pay and all her sisters played,
And Lord Poseidon called:
    'Good-day!
    Good-day!'

    Bliss cannot last.
A '. . . day!' was on His lips, when (as a gull)
Athena landed on His chariot-rail, and said:
    'Without your help the Greeks will lose.'
And so He turned His six towards Troy.

On 12 May 2004, CL wrote to Paul Keegan: 'I have been working on this and that passage of *Big Men* (etc). This for Poisedon [*sic*] – after he has been persuaded to enter the battle on the Greek side by Athena.' The text above then follows. An earlier note to the author himself, in pencil, promises 'a whole section of Pos' ride, a "big" moment'; and he certainly makes more of it than Homer does.

Among several textual variants is a typed version of these lines, sent to Mick Imlah, poetry editor at the *Times Literary Supplement*, sixteen days later, where 'Catalina rainbow-fish precede' replaces 'Californian rainbow-fish fly by' in line 12, and some extra titles – 'the Duke', 'Grand Admiral Marine' – are thrown in here and there for Poseidon.

Beside a lake beneath Mount Ida's head
Delicate hands dry God.

Stumbling in Her peep-toe platforms,
Enter Queen Hera:
'Chrysomniphantine Zeus Olympian.'

'My darling wife . . . How nice . . . Sit here . . .'
Stroking the grass.
'Not now. I must see Mummy.
She and that Gee are quarreling again.
I only came to ask if I could go.'
'Even on our wedding day you did not look so eatable.'
'But Mummy needs me.'
'So do I.' His hand. Her hand.
'It's not just Mummy. Please. Please.
Why are you so demanding at a time like this?'
'I promise you can go. But not just yet.
You are so beautiful. More beautiful than Dia – Ixion's wife –
I had her half-an-hour before she reached the altar-rails.
Quite a day. The Centaurs – Ixion's favourites –
Raped all the guests: men, women, children, dogs, the lot . . .'
'Um . . .'
'And not long afterwards I had Europa, Phoenix' child.
Me as a bull. The upshot there – the King of Crete, Lord
    Minos . . .'
'Um . . .'
'Then came my Lady Semélee, King Cadmus' wife.
Superb – albeit a human – saw me, grabbed me,
And almost stripped my prick down to a thread.
The upshot: Dionysus . . .'
'Um . . .'

'Then there was Alkemene – somewhat coy –
So I possessed her as her husband, duke Amphitrion.
The upshot: Hercules!'
　　'Um . . .'
　　'Then, let me see, ah! yes! my brother Lord Poseidon's best,
Demeter, large, ready, smooth. I had her as a horse, I'm not
　　　sure why
But that is what it took.'
　　'Um . . .'
　　'And then came Leto who I know you know –
Your having chased her all around the north Aegean.'
　　'Um . . .'
　　'Then – happily – your self. My best of bests ' –
Giving her bum a slap –
'So strip your silk, then off you go to Mummy.'

　　[. . .]

And presently God slept.

The bulk of the text here is taken from two pages of ink MS with
pencilled corrections, some of the middle section duplicated, but
with inconsistencies, suggesting two variant texts amalgamated in
a spirit of makeshift. So this is an editor's best shot at reconciling
the two. The final line is from a third page, a rougher sketch of the
same incident.

[*Iliad*, Book 21]

Alaska, 1974.
Think of the moments when
A 50-foot-high cliff of ice
Collapsed into the River Noa'tak,
And by the half-a-day it took to reach the sea,
Its flow – according to the tide-mark that it left –
Became a wave some 1500 metres high
That stripped the land on either side of it
Down to the rock.

Likewise that [. . .]

Various try-outs of this passage are to be found on an MS page with the heading 'A's entry into the fighting'. Confusingly, a more finished draft, the one above, appears after the passage 'Behold the ordered army of the stars!', which refers to events long before Achilles has returned to the fray. Possibly, CL regarded this extended metaphor as opportunistically adaptable, but the MS page just mentioned supports assigning it to the moment early in Book 21 where, after his one-to-one confrontation with Aeneas, Achilles enters on a wholesale slaughter of lesser Trojans, for which Homer provides a completely different simile.

'From a duck's egg, a duck. Doubtless his relative Scamander
Will cleanse this dead, wet, wreck of an obstinate man.
A River king came in his mother's mother's slit so, proud of it,
He went for me, the one plain King's grandchild, and got killed.
But the axioms commemorating divine peerage, state:
Children from Heaven's one plain King – like me, dead man –
Match above any River's boy exactly as
Above the world's rivers combined at their spring estuaries,
Stands Heaven, stands in Heaven, God.
Consider the Scamander, here. A fine example for any River.
A big River. Surely Scamander would have, if he could have,
Taken your part? Pah! . . . I hunt a hare with a drum.
Such opposites mock competition, yes, the Freshwater King,
Achelous himself, plus five wide oceans, plus, O –
Plus the whole damp lot, are good as dead
Faced with God's warning thunder.'
                                        Then Achilles,
Leaving the tall enemy with eels at his white fat
And his tender kidneys infested with nibblers,
Pulled his spear out of the mud and waded off,
After the deadman's troop that beat upstream
For their dear lives.
                                Glimpsing Achilles' scarlet plume
Amongst the clubbed bulrushes, they ran, and as they ran
The Greek got seven of them, swerved, eyeing his eighth, and
Ducked at him as Scamander bunched his sinews up,
And up, and further up, and further further still, until
A glistening stack of water, solid, white with sunlight,
Swayed like a giant bone over the circling humans,
Shuddered, and changed for speaking's sake into humanity.
And the stack of water was his chest; and the foaming

Head of it, his bearded face; and the roar of it –
Like weir-water – Scamander's voice:

'Indeed, Greek, with Heaven helping out, you work
Miraculous atrocities. Still, if God's Son
Has settled every Trojan head on you,
Why make my precincts the scupper for your dead inheritance?
Do them in the fields, Greek, or – or do them anywhere but here.
Thickened with carcasses my waters stiffen in a putrid syrup,
Downstream, the mouth cakes against standing blood-clots yet,
And yet, you massacre. Come, Greek, quit this loathsome
        rapture!'

                        Head back, Achilles cried:
'Good, River, good – and you shall have your way . . . presently.
When every living Trojan squats inside his city's wall.
When I have done with Hector, Hector with me, to death.'
                        And he bayed and leapt –
Bronze flame shattering like a divine beast –
Pity the Trojans!

                        So Scamander
Tried involving the Lord Apollo, thus:
                        'Lord, why the negligence?
Is this the way to keep your Father's word?
Time and again he said: Watch the Trojan flank
Till sundown comes, winds drop, shadows mix and lengthen,
War closes down for night, and nobody is out
Bar dogs and sentries.'

                        Hearing this
The Greek jumped clear into the water and Scamander
Went for him in hatred: curved back his undertow, and
Hunched like a snarling yellow bull drove the dead up
And out, tossed by the water's snout on to the fields;

Yet those who lived he hid behind a gentle wave.
Around the Greek Scamander deepened. Wave clambered
Over wave to get at him, beating aside his studded shield so,
Both footholds gone, half toppled over by the bloodstained
        crud,
Achilles snatched for balance at an elm – ah! – its roots gave –
Wrenched out – splitting the bank, and tree and all
Crashed square across the river; leaves, splintered branches
And dead birds, blocking the fall. Then Achilles wanted out.
And scrambled through the root's lopsided crown, out of the
        ditch,
Off home.

   But the river Scamander had not done with him.
Forcing its bank, an avid lip of water slid
After him, to smother his Greek breath for Trojan victory.
Aoi! – but that Greek could run! – and put and kept
A spearthrow's lead between him and the quick,
Suck, quick, curve of the oncoming water,
Arms outstretched as if to haul himself along the air,
His shield – like the early moon – thudding against
His nape-neck and his arse, fast, fast
As the black winged hawk's full stoop he went –
And what is faster? – yet, Scamander was nigh on him,
Its hood of seething water poised over his shoulderblades.
Achilles was a quick man, yes, but the gods are quicker than
        men.
And easily Scamander's wet webbed claw stroked his ankles.

   You must imagine how a gardener prepares
To let his stored rainwater out, along
The fitted trench to nourish his best plants.
Carefully, with a spade, he lifts the stone
Gagging the throat of his trench, inch by inch,
And, as the water flows, pebbles, dead grubs,

Old bits of root and dusts are gathered and
Swept along by the speed of it, until
Singing among the plants, the bright water
Overtakes its gardener and his control
Is lost. Likewise Scamander took Achilles.

Each time he stood, looking to see which Part, or whether
Every Part of Heaven's Commonwealth was after him,
The big wave knocked him flat. Up, trying to outleap
The arch of it, Scamander lashed aslant and wrapped his
    knees
In a wet skirt, scouring the furrows so his toes got no grip.
And Achilles bit his tongue and shrieked: 'Father . . .'
Into the empty sky '. . . will Heaven help me? No?
Not one of you? Later, who cares? But now? Not now. Not
    this . . .
Why did my lying mother promise death
Should enter me imaged as Lord Apollo's metal arrowheads?
Or Hector, my best enemy, call Hector for a big hit
Over Helen's creditors, and I'll go brave.
Or else my death is waste.
Trapped like a pig-boy beneath dirty water.'

                        In Heaven, two heard him:
First, the woman Prince, Athena; and with her came
Fishwaisted Poseidon, Lord of the Home Sea.
And dressed as common soldiers they came strolling by,
And held his hand, and comforted him, with:
'Stick, my friend, stick. Swallow the scare for now.
We're with you and, what's more, God knows it, so
Stick. This visitation means one thing – no River
Will put you down. Scamander? . . . He'll subside. And soon.
Now child, do this: Keep after him no matter what.
Keep coming, till – I use your own fine words –
Every living Trojan squats inside his city's wall

And Hector's dead. You'll win. We promise it.'

    So the Greek, strong for himself, pushed by, thigh deep,
Towards the higher fields, through water
Bobbing with armoured corpses. Sunlight glittered
Off the intricate visions etched into breastplates
By Trojan silversmiths; and Trojan flesh
Bloomed over the rims of them, leather toggles sunk
To the bone. Picking his knees up, Achilles, now
Punting aside a deadman, now swimming a stroke or two,
Remembered God's best word and struck
Like a mad thing at the river. He beat it
With the palm of his free hand, sliced at it,
At the whorled ligaments of water, yes, sliced at them, Ah! –
There, there – there, and – *there* – such hatred,
Scamander had not thought, the woman Prince,
Scamander had not thought, and now, slice, slice,
Scamander could not hold the Greek! Yet,
Would not quit, bent, like a sharp-crested hyoid bone,
And sucking Achilles to his midst, called out:
'Simois, let's join to finish off this Greek – What's that?
Two against one, you say? Yes. Or Troy is ash,
For our soldiers cannot hold him. Quick, and help, come
Spanned out as a gigantic wave, foot up to peak
A single glinting concave welt, smooth, but fanged
Back in the tumultuous throat of it, with big
Flinty stones, clubbed pumice, trees, and all
Topped by an epaulette of mucid scurf to throttle,
Mash each bone, and shred the flesh and drown away
The impudent who plays at God.
Listen, Simois . . . Nothing can help him now.
Strength, looks – nothing. Why, that heavy armour, how
It will settle quietly, quietly, in ooze,
And his fine white body, aye, slimy and coiled up
I'll suck it down a long stone flue,

And his fellow Greeks will get not one bone back,
And without a barrow to be dug can save their breath for
    games.'

                          And the water's diamond head
Shut over Achilles, locked round his waist
Film after film of sopping froth, then
Heaved him sideways up while multitudinous crests
Bubbled around his face, blocking his nostrils with the blood
He shed an hour before.

                         Then Hera, Heaven's queen,
Looked over the cloudy battlements of Paradise
And saw it all and saw the Greek was done and cursed
    Scamander,
Turned to Hephaestus her son, balanced on a silver crutch
And playing with a bag of flames, who, when his mother
Beckoned with her head, came close and listened:
'Little Cripple, would you fight Scamander for me?
Yes?' – rumpling his hair – 'You must be quick or' –
Giving him a kiss – 'Achilles will be dead. So,
Do it with fire, son; an enormous fire, while' –
Twisting his ear a bit – 'I fetch the white south wind to thrust
Your hot nitre among the Trojan dead, and you must
Weld Scamander wet to bank – now! But . . .
Wait. Little One, don't be talked out of it, eh?
More gods are threatened than struck, Scamander's promises
Are bought. Now, off with you, and, one last thing –
Sear him, Hephaestus, till you hear me shout!'

                        And the Fire God
From a carroty fuse no bigger than his thumb,
Raised a burning fan as wide as Troy
And brushed the plain with it until
Scamander's glinting width was parched

And smoke stopped sunlight.

                              Then the garnet-coloured bricks
Coped with whitestone parapets that were Troy's wall,
Loomed in smoky light, like a dark wicket bounding
The fire's destruction.
Troy's plain was charred and all in cinders
The dead Trojans and their gear. Yet Heaven's Queen
Did not call her son, and the Cripple
Turned on the beaten river.

                              Flame ate the elms,
Sad-willow, clover, tamarisk and galingale – the lot.
Rushes and the green, green lotus beds crinkled – wet dust,
The eels and the pike began to broil.
Last of all, Scamander's back writhed like a burning poultice,
Then, reared up, into a face on fire:
'How can I fight you, Cripple? Flames in my throat,
My waters griddled by hot lacquer! Quit – and I'll quit.
As for Troy and Trojans – let 'em burn. Are not we gods
Above the quarrels of mere humans?'

    You must imagine how the water
    For boiling down the fat of a juicy pig
    After the women pour it into a cauldron,
    Seethes and lifts as the kindling takes
    And the iron sits in a flamy nest.
    Likewise Hephaestus fixed Scamander.

    So the River God called to Heaven:
    'Queen, why does your boy pick on me?
    What of the other Gods who side with Troy?
    I promise to leave off if *he* leaves off. What's more
    I swear to turn away when Troy is burnt by Greeks.'

So she called the Cripple off.

And between his echoing banks
    Scamander
Rushed gently over his accustomed way.

The text here is taken entirely from CL's *Selected Poems*, in spite of the fact that a significantly different version, photocopied from *Songs* (1959), with deletions and corrections in the author's hand, is pasted into 'CONT. PLAN 3'. The problem for the editor was to decide which version was the more recent – impossible to do with absolute certainty. It could have been that CL was dissatisfied with the text as it had appeared in *Selected Poems* and wanted to take another long run at it, using a very early state as starting-point; equally, he may have put it into 'CONT. PLAN 3' purely for the historical record. In the end, I favoured the latter interpretation, not least because in a number of respects it conforms more closely to the style of the rest of *War Music*.

In *Selected Poems*, the episode is prefaced as follows:

'As they returned towards the river Scamander, Achilles split the Trojan army: one half, chased back along the same lines the Greeks had taken yesterday when Hector split their front, ran over the fields towards Troy; the other half were sealed into a loop made by the Scamander.

'Jammed close, these miserable troops slithered down the bank into deep water, screaming as they twisted away from each other, their weapons tangled up, hands snatching at chin-straps.

'Into this confusion Achilles waded, hacking amongst the mass till his arms went numb and the Scamander ran like the gutter set in the floor of a slaughterhouse.

'Up to this time the river had not taken sides: now, soiled by a Greek, Scamander began contriving ways to help the Trojans.

'Such thoughts might well have come to nothing. But, while the river planned, Achilles speared Asteropaeus – the grandson of the river Axius – scooping in the man's belly till his vitals floated out

like mauve welts along Scamander's bank. And not content with
this, Achilles stripped his victim, stood on his chest and said:'

[*Iliad*, Book 22]

Bleak sunlight.

Western Ilium:
Its hills, the sea, Troy in between them, and,
Like shining tidal water, Greece approaching it.

The Trojans close their gates;
Exhausted; safe; resting their backs against the inside of the
     Wall.

Between the city and the sea,
Apollo to Achilles:

'Boy,
Has Hector being Hector blinded you to me?
  I saw no womb. Mix with your dying kind.'

'One prayer of mine,' Achilles said,
'Passes a hundred Trojan templesful
Shitting themselves while on their knees to You,
As You, stripped of your immortality, would go
Down on Your knees to beg Your life from me,
Lord of the Morning Light,' Achilles said.
  Then flicked his reins, and drove,
Eager to kill, across the yellow sand.

Troy.

The acropolis.

Priam, its King, his heart
Heavy enough without this more,
Saw lord Achilles overtake the Greeks.
    Then looking down, this more again:
Hector, his son; his leading son; the son [on] whose worth,
Which is to say, whose courage, strength, and strength of
    leadership,
Troy, Ilium, his kingship, and his family's life, depends,
Step through the great gate's wicket gate,
A javelin in one, and in his other hand
A helmet and a posy shield,
A sheathed sword slung across his back,
And close the gate behind him.

    Again

    All is so still

    So still

    The old man has no need to raise his voice:

    'Hector.
Come in.
    The Greek will kill you . . .'

    Who draws near

    '. . . Then me.'

    Quite near . . .

    'And then your son.'

And then he slowed.

And then he stopped.

Unambiguously placeable at the beginning of Book 22, in which Achilles settles his score with Hector.

[*Iliad*, Book 22]

In brilliant sunlight, the plain of Troy.
The Great Wall of Troy.
Thunder. The kind that sounds like cloud-sized snooker balls
    knocking together.

   'The Greeks are coming!'

Hector alone outside the Skean gate.

Lines in isolation and at a very early stage of drafting, in MS they present a muddle of second thoughts and crossings-out, in ink first, then pencil; but their purpose in building up tension before the combat between Hector and Achilles is clear enough.

No doubt, when you were young,
You came across a person or a thing
That made the meaning of the word *big* clear.
Seeing Achilles is like that: plus, of course,
His bigness is exceptionally beautiful.
You are obliged to stand and stare.
Likewise Prince Hector stood, and as he did
His legs began to shake; and then his body.
And his arms began to shake; and then, the shame of it,
His hair stood up; his teeth began to chatter in his head;
Then, the Wall immediately behind him, he
Arms out, his hair streamed out, between –
One hot, one cold – King Laomedon's sacred springs, he ran
Fast as a beam of light through falling snow
Toward the Gates, towards its wicket, then through the Wall:
Except he did not reach the Gates; he had to turn and start
A slightly shorter run, a little nearer to the Wall,
But still some distance out from it, because
Achilles reached, and turned his turn
Although it was a little further in
Back on itself; so Hector turned, and tried again,
This time a little further in, but still
A distance out from it; and then again,
This time still closer in, three yards,
That is to say, nine feet from it.
Then he stopped.

Far as it is from completion, this is the page where CL's various attempts to get started on the actual fight between Hector and Achilles go furthest. Most of the MS is in pencil, just the first seven-and-a-half lines being inked in, and CL breaks off a first draft to take a second stab at the passage beginning 'Towards the Gates . . .'.

Sunset.

    Greece to its ships to eat and sleep.
But Achilles could not sleep
Because he could not stop himself
Thinking about Patroclus.
    How in this war or that
They saved each other's lives a dozen times a day,
Or how rash words died in him at Patroclus' glance.
    He tried this side, then that.
Then he got up and went down to the beach,
Refettered Hector's ankles to his chariot's step,
And galloped the cadaver – kept from harm by visitant hands –
Round and around the embers of his true heart's pyre.
Crying his eyes out.

Twelve days of this.

Then

God to His gods:

    'Hector kept faith with us:
Regular bloodshed: frequent prayers.
He dies. His body is defiled. And Heaven does nothing.
Achilles can do what he likes with you.
Thousands have lost as much again as he has lost.
Grief has its term. I will not have existence hissed.'

    'Darling,' – His wife, Queen Hera, said –

'Hector is just another animal. Contrarywise,
Achilles' mother – as you know very well –
Is one of Us. He has immortal genes then? Yes?
Not a full set, agreed. Nevertheless
All Paradise – including You – came to their wedding.'
  'A memorable event.'
  'Thankyou, Athena.'

  'That is enough,' God said.
'Hector will have a royal end.
  Iris?'

  There is a cave in Samothrace
Whose mouth is screened by fragrant leaves.
Here Iris found Achilles' mother, Thetis,
Worrying about her son while gazing out
Across the still, Aegean sea,
And took her hand, and spoke to her by name.

  'God calls.'
  'I am too sad to look Him in the face,' she said,
But put a shawl blue as the sky around her shoulders, then her
    head,
And went.

  Alone with God.

  'Thetis, tell your son grief has a pause.
See that he eats, then has a girl.
Remind him he is due to die quite soon,
And he must stop fouling Prince Hector's corpse.'

She goes.

Then:

'Iris.'

'Sire?'

'Visit Troy. Tell its King:
You are to bring your son's corpse home.
Its ransom – large. Appropriate.
Go now. Alone, save for your driver.
You will be treated with respect.'

Troy.

'King,' Iris said,
You are to bring your son's corpse home.
Its ransom – large. Appropriate.
Go now. Alone, save for your driver.
You will be treated with respect.'

'You will be killed,' his wife, Hecuba, said.
'God put Achilles on this earth to kill.
His name means kill.
He killed my Hector. He will kill you.
Each morning I go down onto my knees
Begging the Lord to let me strangle him,
Then butcher him, then boil, then eat his heart.
Remember Hector. My brave boy.'

The Treasury.

Its chests.

Their painted lids.

The gifts:

    12 cloaks, each with a stitch-worked hunting scene.
12 soutanes, cut from white silk, with silvered hems.
12 lots of butter-coloured, Irish gold.
An amber chalice rimmed with platinum –
A wedding gift from Tirium of Cos.

The Citadel.

    Carrying a cloth of gold,
Weeping, and at the same time, laughing,
Watched by his wife, his wives, his teenaged sons,
Using his cane on anyone who came too close,
The old king helped himself into his cloak,
Reached for his driver's hand and hub-stepped up
Onto the flat-topped transport; knelt, face cowled
Among his crated gifts, and prayed:

    'Great Lord and Master of the Widespread Sky,
    Grant that the Greek accepts my words, my gifts.'

As he was driven down the Skean road
Towards Achilles and the sea.

N o moon.

Then,

Torchlight on points

On masks.

Hands move the old king onto a litter.

Then he is gone.

T o reach the curtains that divide
The inner from the outer areas of lord Achilles' tent,
You take the three steps up
Onto a stage of jointed planks that lead to them
Beneath a sailcloth canopy.

   Beside these steps they parked King Priam's litter,
Where, but above him, lord Achilles, waiting, let
The old king get himself up out of it
Onto the stage, and, kneeling, kiss his hands:
The hands that killed his son.

   A pause.

   Then they go in.

   'I shall not sit,' King Priam said,
'While my son Hector's body lies outside
Dirty and bare.
Accept my gifts. Give me my son's body. Let me go back to Troy.

And you go back to Greece. With gold.'

'That is enough from you,' Achilles said, and then –
After a pause –
   'The corpse is yours. You will sleep here. But out of sight.
The Greek kings often come to me.
One sees you, up goes the body's price.
   'Automedon?'

   'My Lord?'

   His bed is made.
Likewise his driver's.
Everybody sleeps.

Iris to Priam in a dream:

'Leave now.'

   And while he shook his driver,
Yoked their mules, bolted their tail-gate,
As silently as if her hands were air,
The harness, air,
So no one heard them leave,
Or saw them as they drove away,
Then reached, and crossed,
Just as the sun came up,
Scamander's ford,
With Hector's body by the tail-gate
Wrapped in the cloth of gold.

AUTHOR'S NOTES

The 'Notes' that Christopher Logue added to *The Husbands* (1994) and all his subsequent Homer volumes throw light on the range of allusion embedded in them. It is evident that in compiling them he often relied on inexact memory, and the presentation of references varies from volume to volume; so some attempt has been made below to correct, to clarify and to lend a measure of stylistic unity. CL's own copy of the 2001 *War Music* includes, as well as textual corrections, jottings in his hand that would probably have formed the basis of notes to any reprinting, and as many of these as possible have been included.

KINGS

16 'soft-topped-eyed': cf. Vincenzo Catena, *Virgin and Child with Mary Magdalen and a Female Saint (Catherine?)*, Glasgow Museums.

20 'Like two bald men fighting over a comb': cf. S. G. Champion, *Racial Proverbs*, 1963, p. 256; also, Christopher Smart, 'The Two Bald Men', *A Poetical Translation of the Fables of Phaedrus*. A very popular proverb.

21 'backlit by long-necked flames': cf. Dryden, 'Annus Mirabilis', stanza 234.

29 'Imagined more than seen': cf. Tennyson, *The Princess*, 'Conclusion', l. 48.

31 'part dust, part deity': cf. Byron, *Manfred*, Act I, Scene ii, l. 40.

337

91 'With blank, unyielding imperturbability': cf. David
   Gascoyne, 'The Bomb-Site Anchorite', l. 20, in *An*
   Enitharmon Anthology, ed. Stephen Stuart-Smith, 1990.

92 'who was no prisoner': cf. Chaucer, *Troilus and Criseyde*,
   Book 4, stanza 26.

96 'Murat': Joachim Murat, King Joachim I of Naples,
   Napoleon's principal cavalry commander.

97 'your voice is like an axe': cf. Bertrand Barère de Vieuzac,
   Memoirs (trans. De V. Payen-Payne, 1896), Volume 4, p. 336,
   where he says of Saint-Just's [Louis-Antoine de Richebourg
   de Saint-Just's] reports to the National Convention, 'they
   spoke like an axe'; given as 'He spoke like an axe' by Ian
   Hamilton Finlay and Richard Healy on their *card*, 1984.

99 'cool their hooves': cf. Chapman, *Iliad*, Book 3, ll. 339–40.

101 'coclackia': a flooring made from pebbles set in mortar;
   also exterior floors so made.

108 'Slack fighting . . . big-lipped wounds . . .': for the first,
   cf. Marie-Louise-Victoire de Donnissan, Marquise de la
   Rochejaquelein, *Memoirs*, 1889 (abridged and translated by
   Cecil Biggane, 1933), p. 288; for the second, Chester Himes,
   A Rage in Harlem, 1985, p. 55.

110 'Where the passing of the day is the only journey' = '*Avec*
   la file des jours pour unique voyage', Jacques Brel, 'Le Plat
   Pays', trans. Rosemary Hill.

112 'can sink them pitilessly': cf. William Carlos Williams, 'The Yachts' (his best poem), l. 5.

125 'Cloud coral in deep seas': cf. Keats, 'To Homer', l. 4.

126 'Each army saw': cf. Shakespeare, *Henry V*, Act 4, Prologue, l. 9.

126 'As through it came . . . a nursing kiss': cf. Tennyson, 'Pelleas and Ettarre', ll. 36–8.

134 'long bronze slope': cf. Tennyson, 'The Charge of the Heavy Brigade at Balaclava', l. 17.

136 'Leave her to Heaven': cf. Shakespeare, *Hamlet*, Act 1, Scene 5, l. 86.

136 '"Beauty," he says . . .': cf. Petrarch, 'Sonnet 61', *Canzoniere*, trans. Robert M. Durling in his *Figure of the Poet in Renaissance Epic*, 1965, p. 73; and Boccaccio, *Filostrato*, Part 3, stanzas 31–3, trans. N. G. Griffin and A. R. Beckwith, 1929.

ALL DAY PERMANENT RED

152 '*I shall be busy . . .*': cf. Sir Jacob Astley's prayer before the battle of Edgehill (Sir Philip Warwick, *Memoirs*, 1702).

156 'Blind as the Cyclops': cf. Dryden's 'Astraea Redux', l. 45.

157 'Blends with the sound . . . circled by poplar trees': Jasper Griffin's translation from Virgil's *Georgics.*

163 'The great gold glittering Limpopo': cf. Rudyard Kipling's *Just So Stories*, 'The Elephant's Child' – 'the great, green, greasy Limpopo'.

165 'All in a moment on T'lespiax' note': cf. Milton, *Paradise Lost*, Book I, l. 544.

166 'I am full of the god!': cf. Pope's *Iliad*, Book XIII, l. 115.

167 'Oh wonderful, most wonderful, and then again more wonderful': cf. Shakespeare, *As You Like It*, Act 3, Scene 2, l. 202.

168 The lines from 'King Ivan Kursk' to 'if we had lost?' derive from John Erickson's *The Road to Berlin: Stalin's War with Germany*, Volume 2, and from Boris Slutsky's *Things that Happened* (poems and notes), translated with commentaries by G. S. Smith.

169 'Flags tossing above agitated forms': cf. Stephen Crane, *The Red Badge of Courage*.

172 'There's Bubblegum!': this passage derives from the opening pages of Louis-Ferdinand Céline's *Guignol's Band*, trans. Bernard Frechtman and Jack T. Nile.

175 The lines from 'Bread trucks have begun to stream' to 'as the sun lights up the east' are from August Kleinzahler's poem 'An Englishman Abroad'.

COLD CALLS

192 'A glow came from . . . betokened the divine': cf. Virgil, *Aeneid*, 1, ll. 589–90, trans. C. H. Sisson.

193 'His head was opened . . . trickling from his mouth': cf. Henry Williamson, *The Patriot's Progress*, 1930, p. 117.

197 'cloudy sunshine': cf. Dryden, 'Beneath a Myrtle Shade',
The Conquest of Granada.

220 'Lord, I was never . . . my father Dad': cf. Shakespeare,
King John, Act 2, Scene 1, ll. 466–7.

WAR MUSIC

229 'October . . . nod': I think that these lines are based on a
translation of Kenneth Rexroth in his *One Hundred Poems
from the Chinese*.

242 'And in the half-light . . . Wavering begins': cf. Pound, 'The
Return', *Ripostes*, 1912.

256 'And all their banners . . .': cf. HD's [Hilda Doolittle's]
poem 'I would forgo'.

268 'Gods have plucked . . .': cf. Dickinson, 'There is a pain – so
utter –', poem 599, *The Complete Poems of Emily Dickinson*,
ed. Thomas H. Johnson.

272 *'Now, now, or never . . .'*: cf. Pound, 'Homage to Sextus
Propertius', V, 1, l.1.

274 'The whole world's woe': I am fairly sure that this comes
from Pope, but I am unsure from whereabouts in Pope.

284 'Soft are her footsteps': cf. Campion, 'Kind are her
answers', *Third Booke of Ayres*, 1601.